FOOD GLORIOUS FOOD

FOOD
Glorious
FOOD

**From cakes to curries
to Cornish pasties –
favourite dishes from the
search for Britain's best recipe**

FOREWORD BY
SIMON COWELL

MITCHELL BEAZLEY

Contents

Foreword

What I love about *Food Glorious Food* – the show, and now this book – is that it's the opposite of all the other food shows and cookery books I've seen before.

I've always believed that the best British food is found on kitchen tables in homes up and down the country, not in fancy restaurants – and that was why we made this series. We wanted to find those special home-cooked dishes and recipes that have been passed down through family generations.

Food Glorious Food has shown that really great home cooking has never been so popular, whether it's the best oatcakes in Stoke-on-Trent or amazing homemade Cornish pasties.

This book is filled with all those special recipes, including my own favourite – Mum's roast potatoes; her recipe for these can be found just below.

To everyone who has opened their family recipe books and shared them with us all – thank you. Thank you for cooking and thank you all for watching.

MUM'S ROAST POTATOES

1.5kg (3lb) large Maris Piper potatoes

olive oil

salt

Preheat your oven to 220°C/425°F/Gas Mark 7. Peel the potatoes, cut them in half and cook in boiling salted water for 10 minutes, until they've just started to go soft. Drain well and let them dry without allowing them to get cold. Meanwhile, pour a generous amount of olive oil into a roasting tin and place in the oven until piping hot. Lay each potato cut side down on a work surface and scrape lines across the tops with a fork. Put the potatoes, cut side down, in the hot oil and place in the oven. Roast for 40 minutes, or until crispy, turning the potatoes during the cooking so that they are golden all over. Season with a sprinkling of salt just before the cooking time is up.

SOUTH-WEST

SOUTH-WEST

The Kingsbridge Show, with the glorious rolling hills of Devon's South Hams as its backdrop, was the setting for the South-West heat. The show was a brilliantly entertaining family day out, with terrier racing, a motorbike stunt display and, to the delight of *Food Glorious Food* host Carol Vorderman, a vintage-tractor parade.

Along with some unconventional recipes, such as Liquid Nitrogen Ice Cream and the deliciously boozy Celebration Cuptails, there was a focus on local produce and local foodie themes. Many contestants included apples or cider in their recipes, reflecting the long-standing link between apples and the West Country. In fact, wassailling – visiting the orchards on 17 January to sing to the apple trees to encourage a good harvest – is an ancient tradition that still goes on today.

As the sun shone down, the cakes and puddings streamed in, much to the delight of judges Anne Harrison, Stacie Stewart, Loyd Grossman and Tom Parker Bowles. And, of course, this is pasty country. Cornish pasties were popular in the 17th and 18th centuries as a portable meal for tin miners and farmers. They could be eaten without cutlery, stayed warm for a long time and were easily heated up on a shovel held over a candle if they got cold. And they are still hugely popular; this heat featured traditional Cornish Pasties, their close relatives, Devonshire Pasties, and some other very untraditional pasties indeed!

SOMERSET CHICKEN

SERVES 4

1 Bramley apple, peeled, cored and sliced

salt and freshly ground black pepper

4 skinless chicken breasts

400ml (14fl oz) medium-dry scrumpy cider

2 medium red onions, cut into wedges

2 garlic cloves, finely chopped

2 or 3 sprigs of rosemary

75g (3oz) breadcrumbs

25g (1oz) Parmesan cheese, freshly grated

leaves from 4 sprigs of thyme

75g (3oz) mature Cheddar cheese, grated

2 tbsp olive oil

Preheat the oven to 180°C/350°F/Gas Mark 4.

Place the apple slices in 4 rows inside a baking dish (I use an oval dish measuring 35 x 24 x 6cm/14 x 9½ x 2½in).

Season the chicken breasts and rub it in well. Place atop the apple rows, folding in any elongated ends to ensure the breasts are plumped up and all the same size. Pour three-quarters of the cider over and around chicken and allow to marinate for 10 minutes.

Add the onions and garlic to the dish along with the rosemary sprigs and remaining cider (it should come about halfway up the chicken now). Place in the oven for 20 minutes, or until the onions are tender.

Meanwhile, blitz the breadcrumbs in a blender or food processor. Add the Parmesan, thyme and a pinch of salt and pepper, then tip on to a plate.

Carefully make a lengthways incision in the side of each of the cooked chicken breasts to create a pocket. Sprinkle the Cheddar inside and on top of each breast, cover generously with the breadcrumbs and pat down. Drizzle with the olive oil and return to the oven for another 20 minutes, until the topping is crisp. If this fails to happen, transfer the chicken to a shallow baking tin and grill for a few minutes to crisp up.

Serve the chicken with herby roasted new potatoes or crunchy-skinned jacket potatoes, plus some greens – preferably green beans and broad beans cooked with pancetta and garlic.

Eunice Woolcock has been making Cornish pasties for almost 90 years. She learned to make them from her mother when she was a little girl, just as her mother had learned from her mother. Eunice has won many awards and accolades for her Cornish pasties at local shows, and has handed the recipe down to her daughters, grandchildren and even her great-grandson.

CORNISH PASTY

SERVES 1

1 small potato, quartered and thinly sliced

25g (1oz) turnip, thinly sliced

125g (4oz) steak or beef skirt, cut into small pieces

salt and pepper

⅛ onion, sliced

For the pastry
125g (4oz) plain flour, plus extra for dusting

25g (1oz) lard, cubed

25g (1oz) margarine, cubed

50ml (2fl oz) cold water

1 tbsp milk or beaten egg

Preheat the oven to 180°C/350°F/Gas Mark 4. Line a baking sheet with baking parchment.

First make the pastry. Place the flour in a mixing bowl, add the lard and margarine and rub together with your fingers until an even crumb is achieved. Slowly add the water, stirring constantly, until a soft dough is formed.

Lightly flour a work surface and roll the pastry into a circle about 20–23cm (8–9in) in diameter. Place three-quarters of the potato in a layer on one half of the pastry. Top with the turnip, then the beef, and season generously. Add the onion and finish with the remaining potato. Fold the pastry over and crimp along the side, ensuring there are no gaps for any juices to bubble through. Pierce a small slit in the top of the pasty and brush the top with milk.

Place the pasty on the prepared sheet and bake in the middle of the oven for 45–50 minutes. Eat hot or cold.

MARY'S BACON CLANGER

SERVES 4

250g (8oz) self-raising flour

1 tsp baking powder

125g (4oz) suet

about 300ml (½ pint) water

1 onion, diced

5 rindless rashers of smoked bacon, chopped

1 tbsp mixed herbs

butter, for greasing

freshly ground black pepper

Sift the flour and baking powder into a bowl, then add the suet. Gradually mix in the water to form a dough. Place it on a lightly floured work surface and roll into a rectangle about 5–10mm (¼–½in) thick. Cover with the onion and bacon, sprinkle over the mixed herbs and season with pepper to taste.

Roll the pastry up from the short side, rather like a Swiss roll. Place a sheet of baking parchment about 40 x 50cm (16 x 20in) on a work surface and lightly grease with butter or oil. Place the clanger lengthways on the sheet, bring up the long sides of the parchment and fold them over again and again until the clanger is snuggly enclosed. Now fold the ends of the parchment underneath the clanger to finish the parcel.

Put the clanger into a steamer for 1–1½ hours, until it has roughly doubled in size and the crust is golden. If you don't have a steamer big enough, wrap the parcel tightly in foil and steam in a large pan instead.

Serve the clanger with mashed potato, any vegetables you like, and gravy.

Fisherman Alan Steer is passionate about South Devon crab and wants everyone to enjoy it as much as he does. This recipe is based on a thermidor dish Alan's father used to make while he was growing up. Alan always uses the crabs he catches himself, but if you can't source fresh whole crab try using fresh crab meat baked in large ramekins.

BAKED CRAB
WITH BROWN CRAB BUTTER

SERVES 2

20g (¾oz) butter

½ small onion, finely chopped

½ tsp English mustard

½ tsp horseradish cream sauce

2 tsp lemon juice

85ml (3¼fl oz) double cream

225g (7½oz) white crab meat (shells washed and retained)

50g (2oz) mild Cornish Cheddar, grated

2 tbsp breadcrumbs

1½ tsp finely chopped parsley

salt and freshly ground black pepper

For the crab butter
brown crab meat from 1 crab (about 150g/5oz)

½ tsp horseradish cream sauce

75–100ml (3–3½fl oz) double cream

Preheat the oven to 180°C/350°F/Gas Mark 4.

Melt the butter in a pan over a medium heat and sauté the onion until soft but not coloured. Add the mustard, horseradish and lemon juice, then stir in the cream. Once the sauce is combined, stir in the white crab meat. Spoon the crab mixture into the cleaned shells, place on a baking sheet and bake for 8 minutes.

Meanwhile, combine the cheese, breadcrumbs and parsley in a bowl with a little salt and pepper. Set aside.

To make the crab butter, place the brown crab meat and horseradish in a food processor and whiz together. With the motor running, slowly add the cream until a mayonnaise-like consistency is reached. Decant the mixture into 2 ramekins.

When the crab is cooked, cover it with the breadcrumb mixture and place under a hot grill for 2–3 minutes, or until golden.

Serve the baked crab with hot granary toast and a small dish of crab butter on the side.

Pat Hatton created this tasty pie using herbs from her garden, getting the balance just right so it tasted exactly how she wanted. Everyone who eats it says it's delicious, and if you don't grow your own herbs it'll still be lip-smackingly good with fresh herbs bought from the supermarket.

CHICKEN & LEEK PIE
WITH SAGE & THYME

SERVES 4-6

1 tbsp vegetable oil

1 medium onion, finely chopped

2 garlic cloves, crushed

500g (1lb) chicken breast meat, diced

1 medium leek, halved lengthways and cut into 1cm (½in) slices

25g (1oz) butter, plus extra for greasing

25g (1oz) plain flour, plus extra for dusting

450ml (¾ pint) full-fat milk, plus extra for glazing

1 tbsp chopped sage leaves

1 tbsp chopped thyme leaves

salt and freshly ground black pepper

1 tsp cornflour mixed with a little water (optional)

500g packet of ready-made puff or shortcrust pastry

Preheat the oven to 200°C/400°F/Gas Mark 6. Butter a pie dish (the one I use is 28 x 20 x 5cm/11 x 8 x 2in).

Put the oil in a large non-stick frying pan, add the onion and fry until soft but not browned. Add the garlic and stir over a low heat for 1 minute. Add the chicken, increase the heat and stir-fry until golden on outside. Add the leek, then lower the heat again, stirring occasionally while you make the sauce.

Melt the butter in a saucepan and stir in the flour to make a paste. Gradually mix in the milk, stirring constantly to prevent any lumps. Add the herbs and stir until the mixture thickens.

Pour the sauce over the chicken mixture and season with salt and pepper. Stir the mixture, then bring to the boil and simmer for 5 minutes, stirring occasionally. If the sauce is very thin, quickly mix in the cornflour paste.

Lightly flour a work surface and roll out the pastry to a thickness of 3mm (⅛in) or so. Use just over half of it to line the prepared pie dish. Roll out the remaining pastry to use as a lid.

Working quickly, pour the pie filling into the pastry case and spread it out evenly. Place the lid on the pie and crimp the edges together. Make a small slit in the top of the lid to let the steam out, then brush the surface with milk. Use any pastry trimmings to make decorative leaves if you wish, placing them on top of the pie and brushing with a little more milk. Bake for 30 minutes or until golden brown.

Serve the pie piping hot with either chips and a crunchy salad, or roast potatoes, green beans and carrots.

Zoe Sing uses locally caught fish and seafood to create this dish. She experimented with the recipe with her family, who all enjoy fresh seafood. The pea purée not only tastes great, its bright green hue looks awesome with the other elements of the dish.

ZOE'S SEAFOOD MEDLEY
WITH PEA PURÉE & LEMON MAYONNAISE

SERVES 1

2 raw tiger prawns, peeled

2 tbsp sweet chilli sauce

5cm (2in) piece of fresh ginger, grated

salt and freshly ground black pepper

olive oil for marinating and frying

50g (2oz) chicken skin, excess fat removed

1 small fillet sea bass (about 100g/3½oz), scaled, pin-boned and trimmed

2 tbsp butter

½ lemon

2 scallops, shells and roe removed

250ml (8fl oz) coconut cream

handful of pea shoots

Place the prawns in a bowl with the chilli sauce, ginger, salt and pepper and a drizzle of olive oil, mix well, then cover and leave to marinate for a couple of hours (or even overnight).

Preheat the oven to 180°C/350°F/Gas Mark 4. Line a baking sheet with parchment.

Combine all the lemon mayonnaise ingredients in a bowl and season to taste.

Place the chicken skin on the prepared sheet, fold the parchment over it, then sit another baking sheet on top and place in the oven for 20 minutes, or until the skin is crisp and golden brown. Break into shards and season with salt.

Meanwhile, make the balsamic reduction. Put the ingredients in a small pan and bring to a simmer. Keep simmering for 10–15 minutes.

Place the peas for the purée in a pan of boiling water and cook for 2 minutes. Drain and place in a blender or food processor with the butter and some seasoning, then whiz to a purée. Keep warm.

To cook the sea bass, heat a drizzle of olive oil in a frying pan over a high heat. Season the fish and fry, skin-side down, for 2 minutes. Flip it over, add half the butter and a squeeze of lemon juice and cook for a further 30 seconds. Transfer to a plate and keep warm.

For the lemon mayonnaise
2 tbsp mayonnaise
juice and zest of 1½ lemons
handful of parsley, chopped
handful of mint, chopped
1 tsp maple syrup

For the balsamic reduction
5 tbsp balsamic vinegar
2 tbsp caster sugar

For the pea purée
200g (7oz) peas
50g (2oz) unsalted butter

Heat another drizzle of olive oil in the frying pan over a high heat. Add the scallops and cook for about 1–2 minutes, until golden brown on the bottom. Turn them over, add the remaining butter and a squeeze of lemon juice and cook for a further 30 seconds. Transfer to the same plate as the fish.

Put the coconut cream in a frying pan and bring to a simmer. Add the prawns and their marinade and cook for 2–3 minutes, or until the prawns are pink.

To serve, smear a teaspoon of the pea purée across a plate, arrange the sea bass, scallops and prawns on top. Scatter the chicken skin around them, drizzle over the balsamic reduction, sprinkle with the pea shoots and dot the mayonnaise around the plate. Serve immediately with the remaining coconut sauce in a jug if liked.

Ashley Gamble has adapted a dish her mum used to make to create this recipe, which showcases locally sourced British produce. She always uses Somerset cider and often makes this recipe for her friends and flatmates.

STUFFED PORK FILLET WRAPPED IN SMOKY BACON

WITH A CREAMY SOMERSET SAUCE

SERVES 4

1 pork fillet, about 500g (1lb)

4 medium-sized potatoes, diced

12 rashers of smoked streaky bacon

3 tbsp olive oil

For the stuffing
1 tbsp olive oil

50g (2oz) shallots, diced

1 garlic clove, crushed

25g (1oz) butter

50g (2oz) panko breadcrumbs

½ Pink Lady apple, grated

7 sage leaves, roughly chopped

salt and freshly ground black pepper

1 large egg, beaten

Preheat the oven to 230°C/450°F/Gas Mark 8. Remove the pork fillet from the fridge and allow it to come to room temperature.

Cook the potatoes in salted boiling water until almost cooked but still firm. Drain in a colander and set aside.

To make the stuffing, heat the olive oil in a frying pan. Fry the shallots until soft, then add the garlic and fry for a further 2 minutes. Remove the pan from the heat, add the butter and stir until melted. Combine the breadcrumbs, apple and sage leaves in a bowl. Add the shallot mixture, season to taste, then add the egg and mix until well combined.

To prepare the pork, trim the fillet of any sinew, then make a horizontal incision along one side of the fillet to act as a pocket for the stuffing. Push the stuffing firmly inside.

Place a large sheet of cling film on a work surface and place the rashers of bacon side by side until they form a row the same length as the fillet. Place the fillet across the bacon with the stuffing pocket facing down. Lift the cling film to wrap the bacon tightly

For the sauce

500ml (17fl oz) medium-dry Somerset cider, such as Thatcher's Gold

150ml (¼ pint) double cream

2 tsp soft butter

2 tsp plain flour

1 tsp umami paste

1 tsp elderflower cordial

around the fillet, then discard the cling film. Tie the wrapped fillet at 3 or 4 intervals with kitchen string. Place in a roasting tin 'seam' side down and roast for 20–25 minutes, until the juices run clear when a skewer is inserted in the thickest part of the meat. Cover in foil and allow to rest for 5 minutes before carving.

Meanwhile, pour the olive oil into another roasting and heat in the oven for 2 minutes. Carefully add the potatoes, toss them in the oil and roast for about 20 minutes, turning occasionally, until golden brown.

To make the sauce, heat the cider in a saucepan until reduced by half. Add the cream and heat to reduce by a third. Meanwhile, melt the butter in a separate pan, then stir in the flour to form a paste. Using a balloon whisk, mix the umami and cordial into the cream mixture, then whisk in the flour paste until the sauce thickens. Heat, stirring continuously, for 2–3 minutes.

To serve, carve the rested pork into slices and serve with the potatoes and cider sauce. You can serve with additional vegetables if you wish.

Gillian Kerr and Landa Peace sent their daughters to the same school, and this recipe came from their daughters' cookery teacher, Queenie Newcombe. Landa has updated the original recipe by using Devon cider instead of sherry, adding apples and bacon and making a cobbler topping instead of pastry.

DEVON RABBITY PIE

SERVES 4–6

1 rabbit, jointed

salt and freshly ground black pepper

zest of 1 orange

50g (2oz) plain flour

oil for frying

150ml (¼ pint) chicken or vegetable stock

about 350ml (12fl oz) dry scrumpy cider

large sprig of parsley, finely chopped

handful of sage leaves, finely chopped

1 bay leaf

1 large onion, chopped

2 celery sticks, finely diced

225g (7½oz) smoked bacon lardons

1 Bramley apple, peeled, cored and sliced

Place the rabbit joints in a bowl and cover with water. Add 2 teaspoons of salt and the orange zest, then cover the mixture and refrigerate overnight.

Preheat the oven to 180°C/350°F/Gas Mark 4.

Drain the rabbit and dry with kitchen paper. Season the flour, going easy on the salt because the bacon will add further saltiness, and toss the rabbit in it.

Heat a little oil in a frying pan and brown the rabbit pieces. Using a slotted spoon, transfer them to a flameproof casserole dish and set aside. Add the stock, cider and herbs to the frying pan, stirring to incorporate any remnants from the rabbit.

In a clean frying pan, heat a little more oil and sauté the onion until softened. Add the celery and bacon and sauté until the celery has softened. Pour in the cider mixture, stir well and bring to the boil. Pour the contents of the pan over the rabbit in the casserole, cover tightly and place in the oven for 30 minutes. At that point, add three-quarters of the apple, then return to the oven for about another hour, until the meat is falling off the bone. Lift the meat out of the casserole, discard all the bones and dice the flesh. Increase the oven temperature to 200°C/400°F/Gas Mark 6.

1 tsp cornflour mixed with a little water (optional)

1 tbsp Devonshire clotted cream (optional)

For the sage cobbler
250g (8oz) self-raising flour

½ tsp cream of tartar

60g (2¼oz) butter

90ml (3¼fl oz) milk

handful of sage leaves, chopped

1 egg, beaten

Skim any excess fat off the sauce in the casserole dish, then taste and adjust the seasoning if necessary. If the sauce seems too thin, add the slaked cornflour and heat for a few minutes until thickened. If it seems too thick, stir in some extra cider. At this stage, if you're feeling extravagant, add a dollop of clotted cream. Return the meat to the sauce along with the remaining apple.

To make the cobbler, sift the flour, cream of tartar and a pinch of salt into a bowl. Using your fingertips, rub in the butter until the mixture resembles breadcrumbs. Add the milk and sage and mix briefly to form a rough dough. Place on a lightly floured work surface and roll to out to a thickness of 1cm (½in). Using a round 4cm (1½in) plain cutter, stamp out circles of dough and arrange them on top of the meat. Brush with beaten egg and bake for 10–15 minutes, or until golden.

Binixa Ludlow is passionate about the traditional Gujarati cooking that she teaches. Bini's mum used to cook this dish when Bini was young, and it holds fond memories for her whole family as a dish for special occasions. Like any good curry, it needs to be cooked slowly with lots of love and care.

WEST COUNTRY LAMB & TIGER PRAWN CURRY

SERVES 8

½ tsp salt

½ tsp black peppercorns

1.5kg (3lb) shoulder of lamb, cut into 3.5cm (1½in) pieces

1 heaped tbsp finely chopped coriander leaves, to garnish

3 star anise, to garnish

For the sauce
150ml (¼ pint) vegetable oil

5 cassia bark sticks (each about 5cm/2in long)

2 black cardamom pods

4 green cardamom pods

5 star anise

5 cloves

1 tsp ground fennel

½ tsp coarsely ground black pepper

1 tsp ajwain seeds

16 garlic cloves, finely chopped

2 tsp cumin seeds

4 onions, finely chopped

1 tsp fenugreek seeds

First make the sauce. Heat the oil in a heavy-based saucepan for 30 seconds. Add the cassia bark, cardamom pods, star anise and cloves, and simmer gently until fragrant. Add the ground fennel, black pepper and ajwain seeds, then stir in a quarter of the chopped garlic and brown for 20 seconds (be careful not to let it blacken). Add the cumin seeds, allow to sizzle for a few seconds, then add the onions and fenugreek. Cover and simmer on a low heat for 30 minutes, or until the onions are brown, stirring every 10 minutes. Mix in the ginger and remaining garlic and simmer for 2 minutes. Add the dry spices, bullet chillies, sugar and salt. Stir well and cook for 3 minutes. Drain the aubergine, squeezing out any excess water, add it to the pan and cook for 5 minutes over a low to medium heat, stirring constantly. Cover and simmer for 20–25 minutes, stirring in the coriander stalks halfway through.

Meanwhile, prepare the lamb. Bring a large pan of water to the boil. Add the salt, peppercorns and lamb and stir well. Return to the boil, skim any scum off the surface and continue cooking over a medium heat for 30 minutes. Drain, reserving 600ml (1 pint) of the cooking liquid.

Add the meat to the sauce and stir over a medium-high heat until evenly mixed. Add 525ml (17fl oz) of the reserved liquid, bring back to the boil, then reduce the heat and cover with a tightly fitting lid. Simmer gently for 1 hour, stirring occasionally and adding a little more liquid if it seems dry, but avoid lifting the lid

12.5cm (5in) piece of fresh ginger, peeled and finely chopped

1¼ tbsp ground coriander

1¼ tbsp ground cumin

¼ tsp red chilli powder (optional)

2½ tsp ground turmeric

2½ tsp garam masala

2–3 large green bullet chillies

1 tsp caster sugar

4 tsp salt

200g (7oz) aubergine, finely chopped and submerged in water for 15 minutes

200g (7oz) aubergine, peeled and finely chopped and submerged in water for 15 minutes

6 tbsp finely chopped coriander leaves, stalks reserved

200g (7oz) canned chopped tomatoes

2 tbsp chopped chives

For the garlic prawns
3 tbsp vegetable oil

3 garlic cloves, chopped

375g (12oz) raw tiger prawns, shelled

¼ tsp salt

For the chapattis
375g (12oz) wholemeal flour, plus extra for dusting

1 tbsp vegetable oil, plus a little extra for kneading

190ml (6½fl oz) hot water

butter or ghee for dabbing (optional)

For the cucumber salad
7 cherry tomatoes, quartered

115g (3¾oz) carrots, finely chopped

65g (2½oz) cucumber, finely chopped

50g (2oz) red onion, diced

1–2 tbsp of lemon juice

1 tbsp extra virgin olive oil

salt

more than absolutely necessary. Add the tomatoes and stir through the curry with the coriander leaves and the chives. Simmer for a further 20 minutes.

To prepare the prawns, heat the oil in a frying pan and brown the garlic. Add the prawns and salt and stir-fry for 2 minutes. Tip the contents of the pan into the curry and stir gently. If it is looking a little thick, add 75ml (3fl oz) of the reserved liquid. Simmer gently for a further 10 minutes.

To make the chapattis, place the flour and oil in a bowl and rub together until there are no lumps. Make a well in the middle of the mixture and pour in half the hot water. Mix briefly with a spoon, then knead with your hands for 2–3 minutes to form a soft, smooth dough. If it is too hard, add a little water; if it's too soft, add a little more flour.

Break off pieces of the dough weighing about 25g (1oz) and roll them into balls. Flatten in the palm of your hand and dust with dry wholemeal flour. Cover with a tea towel to prevent them from drying out.

Place a tawa or frying pan on a high heat for 1–2 minutes. Meanwhile, remove a piece of dough from under the tea towel and roll it into a very thin circle. Reduce the heat under the pan to medium-low and add the chapatti. Cook for about 30–60 seconds, until you see small bubbles appear on the surface. Turn it over and cook the other side until it also begins to bubble. Flip the chapatti over again and press lightly around the edges with a clean, dry cloth while turning it and allowing it to puff up. Transfer to a serving dish, brush with butter or ghee (if using), and cover with a tea towel to keep warm. Repeat to make about 18 more chapattis.

To make the cucumber salad, combine the tomatoes, carrots, cucumber and onion in a bowl. Toss with the lemon juice and oil, then add salt to taste.

To serve the curry, sprinkle the star anise and chopped coriander on top of the curry, then spoon on to serving plates. Offer the chapattis and salad separately for people to help themselves.

This Chinese-inspired dish came into being when fishmonger Kevin Little accidentally handed his wife a pack of icing sugar instead of cornflour to coat strips of beef with before frying. The recipe has since evolved to use dark brown sugar, but it remains one of the few red meat dishes they really enjoy.

GINGER BEEF

SERVES 2

4 tbsp olive oil

250g (8oz) fillet steak, cut into 8mm (¼in) strips

1 red pepper, cut into 8mm (¼in) strips

5cm (2in) piece of fresh ginger, thinly sliced

1 medium-hot chilli, halved lengthways, deseeded and thinly sliced

zest of 1 orange

juice of 1½ oranges

3 tbsp dark brown sugar

2-4 tbsp soy sauce

bunch of spring onions, very thinly sliced on the diagonal

Heat the oil in a wok. Add the steak and cook for 1-2 minutes, turning frequently. Add the pepper and cook for another 2 minutes. Add the ginger, chilli, orange zest and juice, sugar and soy sauce to taste, and cook for 30-60 seconds. Set aside and keep warm.

Add the spring onions to the hot wok and stir-fry for 20 seconds, so that they are briefly cooked but remain bright green.

Serve the beef with boiled brown rice, arranging them side by side, and put the spring onions down the middle.

Sarah Langmaid adapted her Iranian friend's recipe to create this dish, which is dairy, gluten and egg free – all foods that Sarah can't eat. Diagnosed with multiple food intolerances in 2012, Sarah has had to radically change her diet, and is keen to help others who face the same predicament. This healthy and delicious dish is a great start.

LAMB, AUBERGINE & SUN-DRIED TOMATO STEW

SERVES 4

leaves from 2 sprigs of rosemary, finely chopped

salt and freshly ground black pepper

2 tbsp light olive oil

750g (1½lb) good-quality lamb neck fillets, cubed

1 large onion, chopped

1 aubergine, diced

2 garlic cloves, finely chopped

1 lamb stock cube, crumbled (I use Knorr's gluten-free ones)

500g carton of tomato passata

125ml (4fl oz) red wine

8–10 sun-dried tomatoes, quartered

Place the rosemary and a large pinch of salt in a non-metallic bowl. Add half the oil and toss the lamb cubes in it. Cover and leave to marinate for about 30 minutes.

Place the lamb in a flameproof casserole dish and brown on both sides over a medium heat for 3–4 minutes. Transfer the lamb to a plate and set aside.

Put the onion and remaining oil in the casserole dish and fry over a gentle heat until softened. Add the aubergine, season with pepper and fry over a high heat until the onion and aubergine start to colour. Add the garlic, browned lamb and its juices and continue to fry until the garlic releases its flavours – about 5 minutes. Add the stock cube, passata, wine and tomatoes. Season to taste, then cover and simmer for 1½–3 hours. It is ready when the meat shreds easily when pressed between your fingers. The longer you cook it, the softer it will become.

Serve the stew with boiled rice and a green salad.

SHREDDED PORK CASSOULET

SERVES 6

1 tbsp olive oil

1kg (2lb) pork shoulder, skin removed

1 red onion, chopped

200g (7oz) smoked bacon lardons

1 garlic clove, sliced

1 bay leaf

175ml (6fl oz) red wine

5g (¼oz) dried mixed mushrooms, soaked in 200ml (7fl oz) boiling water for 20–30 minutes

leaves from 2 sprigs of rosemary, finely chopped

7 large sage leaves, finely chopped

2 sprigs of thyme

400g can of chopped tomatoes

salt and freshly ground black pepper

400g can of haricot beans, drained and rinsed

To serve
1 tsp chopped sage leaves

1 tsp chopped rosemary leaves

Preheat the oven to 180°C/350°F/Gas Mark 4.

Heat the oil in a deep, flameproof casserole dish and brown the pork all over. Transfer the meat to a plate and set aside.

Add the onion and bacon to the casserole dish and fry over a medium heat for about 5 minutes, until the onion is soft and slightly coloured and the bacon crispy. Add the garlic and bay leaf and cook for 1–2 minutes. Increase the heat, pour in the red wine and use a wooden spoon to scrape the sediment from the bottom of the pan. Simmer for a few minutes until slightly reduced.

Drain the soaked mushrooms, reserving the liquid, and chop roughly. Add the mushrooms and herbs to the casserole dish and cook for 1–2 minutes. Stir in the tomatoes and season to taste. Return the pork to the dish and, if necessary, top up the liquid with some of the reserved mushroom water so that it comes three-quarters of the way up the sides of the meat (don't overdo it – the consistency mustn't be too thin). Bring to the boil, then cover and place in the oven for 2½ hours.

When the time is up, add the beans and cook the dish, uncovered, for a further 30 minutes, until the meat is tender and brown on top, and the liquid is reduced and thick.

Lift the pork out of the dish and use 2 forks to shred the meat. Return it to the dish and stir it evenly through the cassoulet. If the consistency needs adjusting, place the dish on the hob and simmer briskly to reduce and thicken the sauce. Alternatively, add more mushroom water if too thick.

Sprinkle with the chopped sage and rosemary before serving.

Sir Benjamin Slade's aunt Freda was addicted to chocolate, so invented this chocolatey version of apple crumble. Although this is a family recipe it hadn't been written down, so Sir Benjamin has had to recreate it with a bit of trial and error and his childhood memories of how it should taste. He now likes to serve it to family and friends, who all wolf it down!

AUNT FREDA'S
MAUNSEL PUDDING

SERVES 6

5 cooking apples, peeled, cored and sliced

75g (3oz) demerara sugar

2 standard Mars bars, cut into squares

225g (7½oz) plain flour

115g (3¾oz) butter, cubed

Preheat the oven to 180°C/350°F/Gas Mark 4.

Place half the apple slices in the bottom of a baking dish (about 1.2 litres/2 pints in capacity) and sprinkle with a third of the sugar. Add half the Mars bar pieces, followed by the remaining apple. Sprinkle over another third of the sugar and add the remaining Mars bar pieces.

Put the flour and butter in a bowl and rub together until the mixture resembles coarse breadcrumbs. Stir in the remaining sugar.

Sprinkle the crumble mix over the apples and bake for 40 minutes, until golden. Serve with custard, cream or ice cream.

Ian 'Spike' Andus is a dancing policeman who loves baking for charity – in fact he has raised over £3,000 for Blind Veterans UK in the last two years. This nostalgic recipe was passed on to Ian by his mum, and he has given it a bit more punch with sherry and mixed spice.

BREAD PUDDING

SERVES 12

400g (13oz) sultanas

300ml (½ pint) sherry

500g (1lb) white bread, finely diced

200ml (7fl oz) cold water

2 large eggs

100ml (3½fl oz) sunflower oil

1 tbsp ground mixed spice

200g (7oz) caster sugar

90g (3½oz) self-raising flour

butter for greasing

icing sugar or cater sugar for dusting

Preheat the oven to 160°C/325°F/Gas Mark 3.

Put the sultanas in a bowl with 100ml (3½fl oz) of the sherry and set aside to soak for 15 minutes. Put the bread in a separate bowl with the water and the remaining sherry and leave this to soak for a couple of minutes, until all the liquid has been absorbed.

Add the eggs, oil, mixed spice and sugar to the sultanas, mix well, then stir in the flour. Add the bread mixture and stir again.

Butter a 20 x 20cm (8 x 8in) baking dish and pour in the bread mixture. Bake for 1¼–1½ hours, turning the dish a few times to ensure even cooking. When ready, the pudding should be evenly risen and springy to the touch. Allow to cool in the dish, then cut into squares and dust with sugar before serving.

Lucy Trevarthen started cooking with her nan when she was little and has been passionate about it ever since. This dish originates from an old handwritten recipe shown to her by her nan, but Lucy has adapted it by using peach syrup, which contrasts well with the cherries.

LUCY'S CHEEKY CHERRY PUDDINGS

SERVES 5

50g (2oz) butter, plus extra for greasing

50g (2oz) caster sugar

1 egg, beaten

50g (2oz) self-raising flour

15g (½oz) glacé cherries, chopped, plus 5 whole ones

pinch of baking powder

1 tsp apricot baking glaze

syrup from a 410g can of sliced peaches

Preheat the oven to 180°C/350°F/Gas Mark 4. Butter 5 small ramekins.

Put the butter and sugar in a bowl and cream together. Beat in the egg, then stir in the flour, chopped cherries and baking powder. Divide the mixture between the prepared ramekins and bake for 15–25 minutes, or until the sponge bounces back when pressed with a finger. Set aside to cool for 15 minutes.

Turn the puddings on to individual serving plates. Put a small dab of apricot glaze on top of each one, then stick a whole glacé cherry on it. Pour a drizzle of tinned peach syrup over the puddings and serve immediately.

VICTORIA SPONGE CUPCAKES

Barry Lewis only started cooking in 2010 when he poached an egg and posted the video on YouTube. He has now posted over 400 videos, many of him cooking with his daughter Phoebe – who has been cracking eggs since she was two! This cupcake recipe is one they enjoy making together, and Barry uses his homemade strawberry jam inside.

MAKES 12 CUPCAKES AND 500G (1LB) JAM

160g (5¼oz) soft butter, plus extra for greasing

160g (5¼oz) caster sugar

3 eggs, beaten

160g (5¼oz) self-raising flour

2 tbsp semi-skimmed milk

275ml (9fl oz) double cream

2 tbsp icing sugar, plus extra for dusting

strawberries for decoration

For the strawberry jam
400g (13oz) strawberries, hulled

340g (11¼oz) jam sugar

15g (½oz) butter

First make the jam. Put the strawberries into a saucepan, mash roughly, then cook over a low heat for 10 minutes. Add the sugar and stir continuously until it dissolves. Add the butter and stir constantly over a high heat until the mixture is boiling and extremely thick. Continue boiling and stirring for 3–4 minutes, then pour immediately into sterilised jars (see Tip, page 57). Seal and allow to cool to room temperature, then refrigerate for a few hours or until set.

Preheat the oven to 180°C/350°F/Gas Mark 4. Butter a 12-hole cupcake tray or line the holes with paper cases.

To make the cakes, put the butter and sugar in a bowl and cream together until light and fluffy. Beat in the eggs, then sift in the flour, stir well, and add the milk. Spoon the mixture into the prepared cupcake tray and bake in the centre of the oven for 20 minutes, or until the cakes are springy to the touch. Set aside until cold.

Pour the cream into a clean bowl and whisk into soft peaks. Gradually sift in the icing sugar, whisking until the cream is thick and can be spooned neatly. Refrigerate until the cakes are cold.

To serve, cut through the cupcakes horizontally – either one cut through the middle, about 2.5cm (1 in) from the base, or, if you want more substantial cakes (perhaps for dads), make a second cut just below the 'lid'. Fill the cuts with different combinations of jam and cream. There's no set rule here, so be creative and have fun. Finish with a dusting of icing sugar and decorate with sliced strawberries.

Part-time nurse, mother-of-four and cake-making business owner Carole Beasley has adapted her grandmother's recipe to create these grown-up cupcakes, which should be enjoyed at every opportunity and on any occasion! Be prepared for a flavour explosion and a feeling of happy yumminess.

THE BEASLEY FAMILY'S CELEBRATION CUPTAILS

MAKES 12

170g (6oz) unsalted butter, softened

170g (6oz) caster sugar

3 eggs

1 tsp vanilla extract

170g (6oz) self-raising flour, sifted

2 tbsp milk (optional)

For the frosting
150g (5oz) unsalted butter

625g (1¼lb) icing sugar, sifted, plus extra for thickening

Preheat the oven to 180°C/350°F/Gas Mark 4. Place 12 paper cases in a muffin tin.

Put the butter and sugar in a bowl and cream together until pale and fluffy. Gradually add the eggs and vanilla extract, beating until the mixture is glossy. Fold in the flour until fully mixed, taking care not to overmix or the cupcakes will be heavy. If the mixture seems too thick, add a little milk to loosen it slightly.

Spoon a heaped tablespoon of cake batter into each paper case in the prepared tin – they should be no more than three-quarters full. Bake in the centre of the oven for 10–18 minutes, or until risen, golden brown and springy to the touch. Transfer to a wire rack to cool completely.

For the raspberry daiquiri flavouring

125g (4oz) raspberries (fresh or frozen)

2 tbsp icing sugar

4 tsp white rum

For the toffee vodka flavouring

115g (3¾oz) condensed milk

4 tsp vodka

For the limoncello flavouring

4 tsp limoncello liqueur

zest of 1 lemon

juice of ½ lemon

For the Irish cream flavouring

4 tsp Irish cream liqueur, such as Baileys

12 chocolate-dipped honeycomb spheres, such as Maltesers, crushed

To make the frosting, cream the butter and icing sugar in a bowl until light, fluffy and suitable for piping. In humid conditions you might need to add more icing sugar to thicken it. The frosting can also be flavoured as follows.

For the raspberry daiquiri flavouring, place the raspberries and icing sugar in a saucepan and heat until reduced to a jam-like consistency. Pass the mixture through a sieve by rubbing it with the back of a spoon, then discard all the seeds. Set aside to cool.

For the toffee vodka flavouring, gently heat the condensed milk in a heatproof bowl set over a saucepan of simmering water. Stir occasionally until it changes to a toffee brown colour. Pour into a bowl and set aside to cool.

Using a cocktail stick, prick several holes in the top of each cold cupcake and divide the cakes into 4 groups of 3. In the first group, spoon ½ teaspoon of rum over each cupcake. In the second group, spoon ½ teaspoon of vodka over each cupcake. In the third group, spoon ½ teaspoon of limoncello over each cupcake. In the fourth group, spoon ½ teaspoon of Irish cream liqueur over each cupcake.

Place equal amounts of the frosting in 4 separate bowls. Fold the cooled raspberry sauce into one portion of frosting and stir in the remaining rum. Add some extra icing sugar, a tablespoonful at a time, until the frosting is thick enough to hold its shape. Spoon or pipe it on to the rum-infused cupcakes.

Fold the cooled toffee sauce into another portion of frosting and stir in the remaining vodka. Add some extra icing sugar, a tablespoonful at a time, until the frosting is thick enough to hold its shape. Spoon or pipe it on to the vodka-infused cupcakes.

Take a third portion of frosting and add three-quarters of the lemon zest, all the lemon juice and the remaining limoncello. Add some extra icing sugar, a tablespoonful at a time, until the frosting is thick enough to hold its shape. Spoon or pipe it on to the limoncello-infused cupcakes and sprinkle with the remaining lemon zest.

Take the final portion of frosting and fold in three-quarters of the honeycomb balls and the remaining Irish cream liqueur. If necessary, add some extra icing sugar, a tablespoonful at a time, until the frosting is thick enough to hold its shape. Spoon or pipe it on to the final group of cupcakes and sprinkle with the remaining crushed honeycomb spheres.

THE BEASLEY FAMILY'S CELEBRATION CUPTAILS

Sheila Biddle's late Aunty May was a legendary cook — and this is Sheila's version of one of her most popular recipes. Aunty May would bake either fruit or coconut and cherry bunloaf, but Sheila likes to put all of the flavours together and drizzle golden syrup over the top when the loaf comes out of the oven.

AUNTY MAY'S BUNLOAF

SERVES 12

175g (6oz) margarine

250ml (8fl oz) milk

250g (8oz) caster sugar

150g (5oz) mixed dried fruit

250g (8oz) self-raising flour

125g (4oz) glacé cherries, halved

1 tsp baking powder

90g (3½oz) desiccated coconut

1 large egg, beaten

golden syrup, to glaze

Preheat the oven to 160°C/325°F/Gas Mark 3. Line a 1kg (2lb) loaf tin with baking parchment.

Put the margarine, milk, sugar and dried fruit into a saucepan and heat until the fat has melted. Set aside to cool.

Place the flour in a mixing bowl and stir in the cherries, making sure they are separated. Add the baking powder and coconut, followed by the egg, then stir in the melted fat mixture.

Pour the batter into the prepared tin and bake for 1 hour, or until a skewer inserted in the centre comes out clean.

Place the loaf tin on a wire rack. While the loaf is still warm, drizzle a generous amount of golden syrup over it. (I usually place a piece of kitchen paper under the wire rack to catch any drips, as this helps with the clean-up afterwards.)

Allow to cool in the tin. Serve the loaf with butter.

In 1983 Sandy Gilbert and her husband bought a former bakery, and as part of the deeds they were required to buy this recipe along with the property (by this time a post office). Sandy used to make the cake at 6 a.m. and it would be sold out by 8 a.m.! She now makes the cake using apples from her own orchard and homemade cider.

SECRET RECIPE
DEVON APPLE CIDER CAKE

SERVES 10–12

500g (1lb) sultanas

300ml (½ pint) cider

375g (12oz) margarine or butter

500g (1lb) brown sugar

4 eggs, beaten

4 Bramley cooking apples, peeled, cored and cut into large chunks

625g (1¼lb) self-raising flour

2 tsp ground mixed spice

Put the sultanas in a bowl with the cider and leave to soak, preferably overnight, but for at least 1 hour.

Preheat the oven to 180°C/350°F/Gas Mark 4. Line a 37 x 27 x 7cm (14½ x 11 x 3in) roasting tin with baking parchment.

Put the fat and sugar into a bowl and cream together. Beat in the eggs, then add the sultanas with the cider and apples, holding your nerve because the mixture curdles. Stir in the flour and mixed spice.

Pour or spoon the cake batter into the prepared tin and bake for 40–50 minutes, or until a skewer inserted in the centre comes out clean.

Turn the cake out of the tin, peel off the parchment and cut into rectangles. Serve hot with clotted cream, custard or Devon ice cream, or serve cold at teatime or on a picnic.

CHOCOLATE &
LIME TART CUPCAKES

MAKES 12

2 eggs plus 2 egg yolks

40g (1½oz) caster sugar

300g (10oz) dark chocolate, broken into pieces

200g (7oz) butter

40g (1½oz) cocoa powder

3 tbsp golden syrup

icing sugar for dusting

For the sweet pastry

250g (8oz) plain flour

125g (4oz) butter, plus extra for greasing

50g (2oz) caster sugar

1 egg

1 tbsp water

For the cupcakes

200g (7oz) butter

200g (7oz) caster sugar

2 eggs

150g (5oz) self-raising flour

40g (1½oz) cocoa powder

Preheat the oven to 180°C/350°F/Gas Mark 4. Butter eight 10cm (4in) loose-bottomed tart tins. Line a 12-hole muffin tin with paper cases.

Start by making the pastry. Put the flour and butter into a bowl and rub together until the mixture resembles breadcrumbs. Add the sugar, then stir in the egg and water to form a soft dough. Wrap in cling film and chill for 30 minutes.

Place the chilled dough on a lightly floured surface and roll out to the thickness of a £1 coin. Using one of the prepared tins as a template, cut around it 8 times and use the pastry circles to line the tins. Prick the base of the tarts with a fork, then line the pastry cases with crumpled greaseproof paper and fill with ceramic baking beans. Bake for 12 minutes. Remove the paper and beans and bake for another 5 minutes to dry out. Set aside to cool in the tins. Lower the oven temperature to 160°C/325°F/Gas Mark 2½.

To make the filling, put the eggs, yolks and sugar in a bowl and whisk until light and fluffy. Place the chocolate, butter, cocoa and golden syrup in a heatproof bowl set over a pan of simmering water, stirring occasionally until melted. Allow to cool for 2–3 minutes, then fold into the egg mixture until fully incorporated.

Fill the pastry cases about three-quarters full with the chocolate mixture and bake for about 12 minutes, or until set. Set aside to cool in the tins for 10 minutes, then remove and transfer to a wire rack. Increase the oven temperature to 170°C/340°F/Gas Mark 3.

To make the cupcakes, put the butter and sugar in a bowl and beat together until light and fluffy. Beat in the eggs one at a time. Sift in

For the frosting
250g (8oz) unsalted butter

500g (1lb) icing sugar

75g (3oz) cream cheese

juice and zest of 1 lime

For the ganache
250g (8oz) dark chocolate, broken into pieces

250ml (8fl oz) double cream

25g (1oz) butter

the flour and cocoa powder and fold into the mixture, taking care not to overmix. Spoon the mixture into the paper cases until three-quarters full, then bake for 18 minutes, or until the cakes are springy to the touch and a skewer inserted into the centre comes out clean. Transfer to a wire rack to cool.

To make the frosting, put the butter in a bowl and beat until soft and pale. Mix in the icing sugar and cream cheese, then add the lime juice and zest. Spoon into a piping bag fitted with a round nozzle, and set aside.

To make the ganache, place the chocolate in a bowl. Heat the cream and butter in a saucepan until they reach boiling point, then immediately pour over the chocolate and stir until melted.

To assemble, hollow out the cupcakes with a knife and fill to the top with the ganache. Pipe a swirl of frosting on top of each cupcake, covering the ganache.

Cut 2 of the chocolate tarts into 6 equal pieces and place a piece on top of each cupcake. (You can use the extra tarts to add to more cupcakes or enjoy them on their own.) Dust the cupcakes with icing sugar and enjoy.

Photographer and blogger Gloria Nicol has adapted her father's cake recipe that always used apples from her uncle Tom and aunt Nora's market garden. Gloria now grows her own fruit and preserves it in jars for use all year round, so always has the ingredients to hand. If you don't have time to make the apple butter, you could use ordinary apple purée instead.

TOM & NORA'S ORCHARD CAKE

SERVES 8

115g (3¾oz) plain flour

pinch of salt

2 tsp baking powder

100g (3½oz) ground almonds

100g (3½oz) butter, cubed

75g (3oz) soft brown sugar

1 large egg, beaten

50ml (2fl oz) milk

2 Golden Delicious apples

For the apple butter
1.25kg (2½lb) Bramley apples, peeled, cored and sliced

125ml (4fl oz) cider or water

150ml (¼ pint) maple syrup

125g (4oz) soft brown sugar

1 vanilla pod, split open lengthways and seeds scraped out

For the apple vanilla syrup
500ml (17fl oz) apple juice

150g (5oz) sugar

1 vanilla pod, split open lengthways and seeds scraped out

2 wide thin strips of lemon peel

First make the apple butter. Place the Bramley apples and cider in a pan, bring to a simmer and cook gently for about 20 minutes, until the apples become fluffy when stirred with a spoon. Add half the maple syrup, the sugar, vanilla pod and seeds and place in a slow cooker for 3–4 hours on High, until the apple has caramelised and thickened. (Removing the lid for the last 30–45 minutes helps excess liquid evaporate.) If you don't have a slow cooker, this process can also be done in a saucepan over a low heat, which will be quicker, but requires constant attention as the apples are more likely to catch. When ready, remove the vanilla pod and leave the apple butter to cool. When cold, stir in the remaining maple syrup. This will make more butter than you need, so store the excess in a sterilised jar in the fridge (see tip, opposite) and make another cake later on. Once the jar is opened, store in the fridge. The butter is also delicious spread on toast.

To make the apple vanilla syrup, place all the ingredients in a saucepan and bring to a simmer, stirring to dissolve the sugar. Boil for 10 minutes, until the syrup has reduced by a third. Remove the vanilla pod and lemon peel. This will make slightly more syrup than you need, but the excess can be used to make a delicious drink when diluted with sparkling water.

Preheat the oven to 190°C/375°F/Gas Mark 5. Butter a shallow 23cm (9in) round cake tin and line the base with baking parchment.

Place the flour, salt, baking powder and ground almonds in a bowl. Add the butter and rub into the dry ingredients until the mixture resembles fine breadcrumbs. Add the sugar, egg, milk and 250g

(8oz) of the apple butter. Mix together with a wooden spoon until just combined, then pour into the prepared tin and level the top.

Peel, core and slice the Golden Delicious apples into 5mm (¼in) rings and arrange them on top of the cake mixture, overlapping them to make a pattern. Brush liberally with the apple vanilla syrup, then bake for 35 minutes. Brush the top again with the syrup and bake for a further 15–20 minutes, until the apple slices are nicely browned around the edges, and a skewer inserted in the centre of the cake comes out clean. Brush the last of the syrup over the cake and set aside until cold or just lukewarm.

Serve the cake as a teatime treat, or as a pudding with the addition of whipped cream sweetened slightly with ginger syrup, or with cinnamon ice cream. (If you would like the apples to be a little more charred, simply pop the cake under the grill for a few moments.)

TIP

To sterilise jars and lids, wash thoroughly in very hot water, allow them to dry, then place in an oven preheated to 140°C/275°F/Gas Mark 1 for about 20 minutes. Remove and leave to cool for 10 minutes before filling them.

CHEESE & PANCETTA SCONES

MAKES 12

sunflower oil for frying

125g (4oz) pancetta

1 medium onion, finely chopped

500g (1lb) self-raising flour, sifted, plus extra for dusting

4 tsp baking powder

pinch of salt

2 tsp mustard powder

150g (5oz) unsalted butter, cubed

200g (7oz) mature Cheddar, grated

2 egg yolks, mixed with milk to make 300ml (½ pint) in total

Preheat the oven to 200°C/400°F/Gas Mark 6. Line a baking sheet with parchment.

Heat a little sunflower oil in a frying pan and gently fry the pancetta until crispy and brown. Use a slotted spoon to transfer to a plate.

Using the same pan, gently fry the onion until just beginning to turn brown. Use a slotted spoon to transfer to the bacon plate.

Place the flour, baking powder, salt and mustard powder in a bowl. Add the butter and rub together until the mixture resembles breadcrumbs. Stir in the cheese, then the cooked onions and the pancetta.

Now it's important to work quickly. Gradually stir in the egg and milk mixture until a ball of dough forms. Place it on a floured work surface and either pat or roll it out to a thickness of about 2.5cm (1in). Using a lightly floured 6cm (2½in) cutter, stamp out as many circles as you can. Recombine the remnants of dough, then roll out again and stamp out more circles. Repeat until all the dough has been used. You should get 12 circles. Place them on the prepared baking sheet, spacing them about 2.5cm (1in) apart so they have room to expand. Bake for 12–15 minutes, until brown.

Cool slightly before serving with butter or, if you want to be truly decadent, clotted cream with a bit of chilli jam.

Shelley Alexander invented this dish to sell in her deli. She found that people didn't like the idea of a savoury muffin, and so the 'scoffin' was born – a cross between a scone and a muffin in both name and nature. Shelley uses local Cornish produce in her scoffins, and they have become enormously popular – selling out every day.

SCOFFINS

MAKES 12

25g (1oz) butter, melted

450g (14½oz) self-raising flour

125g (4oz) Cornish Cheddar cheese, grated

1 tsp sea salt, plus extra for sprinkling

1 tsp coarsely ground black pepper

100ml (3½fl oz) olive oil

150ml (¼ pint) milk

2 eggs, beaten

125g (4oz) green pesto

50g (2oz) pine nuts, lightly toasted

50g (2oz) Parmesan cheese, freshly grated

Preheat the oven to 180°C/350°F/Gas Mark 4. Generously grease a baking sheet with the melted butter.

Put the flour, Cheddar, salt and pepper in a large bowl. In another bowl, mix the olive oil and milk, then beat in the eggs. Add the wet mixture to the dry mixture, then add the pesto and three-quarters of the pine nuts. Mix by hand for 2 minutes, or with an electric whisk on a low speed for about 1 minute, until the mixture comes together. It should be glossy, but not so wet that it will not hold a scone shape.

With floured hands, divide the mixture into 12 equal pieces and shape them into muffin-sized scones. Place them on the prepared baking sheet, sprinkle the remaining pine nuts and the Parmesan on top, and add a small pinch of salt to each one. Bake for 20–25 minutes, or until risen and golden. Set aside to rest for 15 minutes.

Serve the scoffins hot or cold with butter, or with salads or soups, making sure the top of the scoffin hits your tongue first.

SOUTH-EAST

SOUTH-EAST

Brighton's buzzing seafront, warm sunshine and delicious food were three fabulous ingredients that went into the South-East heat. Added to this was a really varied group of contestants, including Morris dancers, a watercress-eating champion, a sumo wrestler, a drag artist, the members of a bonfire society and – proving that a love of cooking is ageless – a bevy of young bakers. Thanks to the wonderful summer weather, contestants and their friends and families could sunbathe in deckchairs in true British seaside style while they waited for the judging.

On the food front, there was a fascinating collection of dishes: regional specialities, such as Sussex Pond Pudding, old-fashioned favourites like Bacon & Onion Suet Pudding, moreish Spiced Lentil Vegetable Cakes, and an apple-based variation on the ever-popular Banoffee Pie, prepared by the daughter of the man who devised the original recipe in 1972. This heat featured an abundance of gluten-free goodies too, so no one missed out on enjoying the results of all that hard work in the kitchen.

Lavender, which is a familiar sight growing in the fields of the South-East, is an unusual ingredient but it featured in many recipes in this heat, including Vintage Lavender & Lemon Blancmange and Lavender & Orange Cake. Other locally sourced ingredients making an appearance were watercress – one of Hampshire's most famous crops – South Downs lamb, locally-brewed ale and apples.

The fabulous Miss G is the drag-queen alter-ego of Andrew Pearce, who also owns a successful bridalwear company, which he runs with his husband Rob. Andrew loves to throw elaborate dinner parties, and these savoury profiteroles make a great starter. He learned to cook from his grandmother, and still has her old recipe book.

CRACKED BLACK PEPPER PROFITEROLES
FILLED WITH PECORINO CHEESE

SERVES 6

oil for greasing

55g (2¼oz) butter

140ml (¼ pint) cold water

70g (2¾oz) plain flour

2 large eggs, beaten

1 tbsp cracked black pepper

salt

For the chutney

50g (2oz) butter

8 onions, chopped

1 red chilli, finely chopped

1 bay leaf

70ml (3fl oz) red wine vinegar

80ml (3¼fl oz) balsamic vinegar

200g (7oz) brown sugar

First, make the chutney. Melt the butter in a saucepan, add the onions and fry, stirring, until soft and translucent. Add the chilli and bay leaf and fry thoroughly, for about 5 minutes. Add the red wine vinegar and cook for about 20 minutes. Next, add the balsamic vinegar and cook for a further 10 minutes, then stir in the sugar and simmer for 20 minutes or until the mixture is thick and sticky. Remove the bay leaf and spoon into sterilised jars (see Tip, page 57). Seal tightly and set aside until completely cold. The chutney can be used immediately, but the flavours will continue to develop as it matures.

Preheat the oven to 200°C/400°F/Gas Mark 6 and place a roasting tin filled with water in the bottom to make it steamy. Oil a baking sheet and sprinkle it with some drops of water.

To make the profiteroles, put the butter and water in a saucepan, heat until the butter melts, then bring to the boil. Add the flour and beat until you have a smooth paste. Remove from the heat and add the eggs a little at a time, beating between each addition, until the mixture is smooth. Stir in the pepper and salt to taste. Spoon

For the filling

25g (1oz) butter

4 spring onions, very finely chopped

200ml (7fl oz) double cream

200g (7oz) pecorino romano cheese, grated

salt and freshly ground black pepper

the choux mixture into a piping bag and pipe the mixture into spheres about 2.5cm (1in) in diameter on to the prepared baking sheet and bake for 15–25 minutes, until the profiteroles are dry and crisp.

To make the filling, heat the butter in a pan, add the spring onions and fry for a few minutes, until soft. Set aside to cool slightly.

Put the cream in a bowl and whisk into soft peaks. Fold in the spring onions and pecorino, making sure that the mixture isn't stirred too much or the cream may separate. Season to taste with salt and pepper. Spoon the mixture into a piping bag, make a small hole in the bottom of each profiterole and pipe in the filling.

Serve the profiteroles on a bed of rocket drizzled with a little balsamic vinegar, and a spoonful of the chutney alongside.

After finishing her degree in Fine Art, Jessica Nicholas travelled extensively in South East Asia, and this pie draws on her culinary experiences whilst away. Jessica adorns her pies with chilli-shaped pastry decorations on top. For a more fiery pie filling, leave the seeds in the Thai red chillies or use more chillies.

CHICKEN THAI PIE

SERVES 6–8

vegetable oil for frying

600g (1lb 2oz) skinless, boneless chicken thighs, cut into chunks

1 medium leek, halved lengthways and sliced

bunch of spring onions, cut into bite-sized pieces

2 onions, thinly sliced

100ml (3½fl oz) chicken stock

400ml can of coconut milk

200g (7oz) carrots, cut into bite-sized pieces

200g (7oz) red pepper, cut into bite-sized pieces

200g (7oz) butternut squash, diced

90g (3½oz) baby sweetcorn, cut into thirds

250g (7oz) button mushrooms

200g (7oz) courgettes, sliced into rounds, then halved

125g (4oz) sugarsnap peas, halved

First make the curry paste. Put all the ingredients for it in a blender or food processor and whiz until smooth. (You could use shop-bought paste instead, but it won't taste as good.)

Heat a little oil in a wok or large saucepan, add the chicken, curry paste, leek, spring onions and two-thirds of the onion and fry for 5 minutes, until the meat is sealed. If the meat starts sticking to the pan, add a little of the stock.

Preheat the oven to 180°C/350°F/Gas Mark 4.

Add the coconut milk and stock to the pan and bring to the boil. Next, add the carrots and pepper, stir for 3–4 minutes, then add the squash, followed by the sweetcorn. Simmer for 3–4 minutes, then add the mushrooms, courgettes, sugarsnaps and remaining onion. Simmer gently for 3–4 minutes, until the liquid has reduced a little.

Meanwhile, mix together the palm sugar, fish sauce, tamarind juice, lime juice and shrimp paste, add to the curry and stir thoroughly. Taste for seasoning, then remove from the heat. Add the holy basil (if using) and, if the mixture needs it, the Thai red chillies.

Ladle the mixture into a 28 x 20 x 5cm (11 x 8 x 2in) pie dish, leaving most of the liquid in the wok (you can serve this separately with the pie if you like).

1 tsp palm sugar

1 tbsp Thai fish sauce

1 tbsp tamarind pulp, thinned to the consistency of juice with recently boiled water

juice of 1 lime (or to taste)

½ tsp dried shrimp paste

bunch of holy basil, chopped (optional)

1–2 Thai red chillies, finely chopped (optional)

plain flour, for dusting

500g packet of ready-made puff pastry

1 egg, beaten

For the green curry paste
4 medium-sized green chillies, deseeded and roughly chopped

2 shallots, roughly chopped

2.5cm (1in) piece of fresh ginger, peeled and chopped

2 garlic cloves, finely chopped

medium bunch of coriander, stalks and roots chopped

2 lemongrass stalks, chopped, or 1 tbsp lemongrass paste

zest and juice of 1 lime

1 green pepper, chopped

8 kaffir lime leaves, torn, or the zest of another lime

1 tbsp coriander seeds, crushed

1 tsp ground cumin

1 tsp black peppercorns, crushed

2 tsp Thai fish sauce

On a lightly floured work surface, roll out the pastry to a thickness of 1.5cm (¾in). Brush the edge of the pie dish with a little beaten egg, then place the pastry over the pie dish, cut off the excess, and press around the edge to seal. Using the point of a knife, make a small hole in the top for the steam to escape. Cut decorative chilli shapes from the pastry offcuts, brush the undersides with a little beaten egg and place these on top of the pie. Brush the whole pie with beaten egg and bake for 20–25 minutes, or until the pastry is golden brown.

Serve the pie either on its own or with the reserved sauce and side dishes, perhaps purple sprouting broccoli or pak choi in the winter or a Thai-inspired salad in the warmer months.

BONFIRE STEW
WITH CANNONBALL DUMPLINGS

SERVES 8

1 tbsp vegetable oil

400g (13oz) smoked bacon, diced

400g (13oz) baby onions, diced

350g (11½oz) carrots, diced

4 celery sticks, diced

2 leeks, diced

6 garlic cloves, roughly chopped

1.5 kg (3lb) South Downs mutton, cut into 5cm (2in) dice

450g (14½oz) self-raising flour

2 tbsp tomato purée

2 tbsp honey

2 star anise

1 red chilli

600ml (1 pint) strong English ale, such as Harvey's Bonfire Boy Ale

2 litres (3½ pints) chicken stock

2 sprigs of thyme

sprig of rosemary

1 bay leaf

salt and freshly ground black pepper

400g (13oz) potatoes, peeled and cut into 2.5cm (1in) cubes

For the dumplings
200g (7oz) suet

50g (2oz) butter

10 sage leaves, chopped

1 tbsp English mustard

75g (3oz) sugar

300g (10oz) oak-smoked sheep's cheese, such as Duddleswell, grated

Preheat the oven to 140°C/275°F/Gas Mark 1.

Heat the oil in a large flameproof casserole dish and brown the bacon. Transfer the bacon to a plate, then brown the onions, carrots, celery and leeks. Add the garlic, fry for 1 minute, then transfer the contents of the pan to the same plate as the bacon.

Tip the mutton into the casserole dish, stir in 2 tablespoons of the flour, the tomato purée, honey, star anise, whole chilli and ale and bring to a simmer. Cook for 5–10 minutes, then add the stock, thyme, rosemary and bay leaf, plus the browned bacon and vegetables. Cover the pan and place in the oven for 2 hours, or until the meat is just tender.

Season the stew to taste, then add the potatoes, put the lid back on and return to the oven for 1 hour, or until the potatoes are cooked. Taste and adjust the seasoning if necessary.

To make the dumplings, combine the suet, butter, remaining flour, sage, mustard, sugar and 200g (7oz) of the cheese in a bowl. Season and add just enough water to form a firm dough. Take golf ball-sized pieces of dough and roll them into balls.

Increase the oven temperature to 180°C/350°F/Gas Mark 4 and arrange the dumplings on top of the stew. Sprinkle over the remaining cheese, then cover the dish and place in the oven for 5 minutes. Remove the lid and cook for a further 15–20 minutes, or until the dumplings have risen and are golden.

Bonfire night in Lewes, East Sussex, is a huge event, and publican Tony Leonard cooks this dish with the South Street Bonfire Society every November 5th at the start of the festivities, serving it in his pub, The Snowdrop Inn. The society was founded in 1913 and the recipe is believed to have been invented by the founding members.

This is the first dish that Janne Cutting-Keyton cooked for her husband Victor, and she now makes it every year on their anniversary. Victor loves the dish as it isn't too 'gamey'. The recipe could be made with chicken breasts if guinea fowl isn't available – the cooking times would be the same.

PAN-FRIED
GUINEA FOWL BREASTS
WITH CARAMELISED APPLE SLICES & WALNUTS

SERVES 4

2 tbsp olive oil

salt and freshly ground black pepper

4 guinea fowl breasts, skin on

2 large Cox's apples, or other eating apples, cored and sliced

30g (2oz) walnut pieces

1 tbsp caster sugar

300ml (½ pint) light game, guinea fowl or chicken stock

60ml (2½fl oz) double cream or crème fraîche

Preheat the oven to 200°C/400°F/Gas Mark 6 and put a roasting tin in to heat.

Heat 1 tablespoon of the oil in a frying pan over a high heat. Season the guinea fowl breasts, then place in the pan skin-side-down and fry for 2 minutes, or until the skin is crispy. Turn over and cook for a further 2 minutes. Transfer the breasts to the hot roasting tin and place in the oven for 10 minutes, or until cooked through. Cover with foil and set aside to rest for 10–15 minutes.

Meanwhile, preheat the grill. Place the frying pan over a moderate heat, add the remaining oil and fry the apple and walnuts for 3–4 minutes, turning frequently, until the apple is lightly browned on both sides and beginning to soften. Place them in a single layer on a baking sheet, sprinkle with the sugar and place under a medium-low grill to caramelise.

Pour the stock into the frying pan and boil rapidly until reduced by half. Take off the heat and stir in the cream.

Remove the skin from the roasted breasts, then slice the meat and serve with the caramelised apple and walnuts and a generous spoonful of the cream sauce.

Penny Ericson-Hawkins developed this nutrient-packed, comforting dish for her husband Simon during his chemotherapy treatment. Motivated by spending weeks in hospital with her husband, Penny set up a website resource called 'chemo canteen' for those undergoing cancer treatment.

SIMON'S PIE

SERVES 4

4 lamb shanks

2 tsp olive oil

375ml (13fl oz) red wine

6 garlic cloves (it's fine to leave them unpeeled)

2 onions, chopped

generous handful of dried mixed herbs

50ml (2fl oz) lamb stock

dash of Sriracha hot chilli sauce

3 bay leaves

2–3 tsp plain flour

100ml (3½fl oz) water

2 x 400g cans of Puy lentils, drained

200g (7oz) shallots, finely chopped

For the topping
1.25kg (2½lb) potatoes, peeled and chopped

salt and freshly ground black pepper

pinch of ground nutmeg (or to taste)

Put the lamb and all the ingredients down to the bay leaves into a slow cooker and cook at a medium heat for 6–8 hours, until the meat is falling off the bone. Alternatively, place in a lidded ovenproof casserole dish and cook in an oven preheated to 140°C/275°F/Gas Mark 1 for 4–5 hours or until tender. Set the meat aside to cool, then strain the sauce through a fine sieve. When the meat is cool enough to handle, strip the meat from the bones, discarding any fat.

To make the topping, place the potatoes in cold water, bring to the boil and cook until tender to the point of a knife. Drain, mash and season with salt, pepper and nutmeg.

Meanwhile, preheat the oven to 200°C/400°C/Gas Mark 6.

Bring the strained lamb sauce to a hard boil for about 2 minutes, then reduce the heat to a gentle simmer. Mix the flour and water to a smooth paste, then whisk into the sauce, ensuring there are no lumps. Bring back to the boil and season to taste.

Place the lentils in the bottom of an ovenproof casserole dish, sprinkle the shallots over them, then place the meat on top. Add sufficient sauce to completely cover the meat, then top with the mashed potato, spreading it right to the edges to prevent the sauce from leaking out. Rough up the surface with a fork, then place in the oven for about 20 minutes, or until golden brown on top. Set aside to rest for 10 minutes before serving.

Builder Sam Batho learned to cook with his mum when he was a little boy. This dish takes the classic chicken wrapped in bacon but brings in additional flavours. Sam started with the watercress and added complementary ingredients to create a flavour-packed but balanced dish.

WATERCRESS & CHEESE-STUFFED CHICKEN BREASTS

SERVES 2

2 chicken breast fillets

2 tsp dried mixed herbs

75g (3oz) Gorgonzola cheese

large handful of watercress, chopped

4 rashers of back bacon

300ml (½ pint) full-fat milk

115g (3¾oz) mature Cheddar cheese, grated

freshly ground black pepper

2 handfuls of mixed salad leaves

Preheat the oven to 200°C/400°F/Gas Mark 6.

Using a sharp knife, make a deep horizontal incision in each fillet to create a pocket. Sprinkle the mixed herbs over the meat, transfer to a non-stick baking sheet and place in the oven for 10 minutes, or until the outside appears cooked.

Put the Gorgonzola and watercress in a bowl and mix together. Spoon the mixture into the pocket of each fillet, then wrap with the bacon and return to the oven for a further 15–20 minutes.

Meanwhile, pour the milk into a small saucepan and heat gently. Gradually add the Cheddar, stirring until it has melted and you have a sauce thick enough to coat the back of a spoon. Add pepper to taste.

Divide the salad leaves between 2 serving plates, drizzle over some of the sauce, then place the chicken parcels on top. Drizzle over the remaining sauce and serve straight away.

Lalita Doig was brought up on traditional Guyanese food, and has developed this dish to combine the flavours of her childhood with locally sourced, sustainable fish and shrimps. She salts her own whiting, which means she can control the texture of the fish – the longer it is salted for, the firmer the flesh and the longer the soaking and cooking time.

LALITA'S COCONUT CURRIED WHITING & SHRIMP GRATIN

SERVES 6

600g (1lb 2oz) whiting fillets, skin on

90g (3½oz) sea salt flakes

50g (2oz) unsalted butter

1 small shallot, finely chopped

1 garlic clove, grated

½ green chilli, finely chopped

2.5cm (1in) piece of fresh ginger, grated

1 tsp curry powder

1 leek, finely chopped

200ml (7fl oz) semi-skimmed milk

50g (2oz) plain flour

400ml can of coconut milk

125g (4oz) cooked brown shrimps

1 tbsp chopped coriander

juice of ½ lemon

salt and freshly ground black pepper

Place the whiting in a shallow dish and cover with the salt. Cover the dish with cling film and place in the fridge for 1 hour.

Melt the butter in a saucepan, add the shallot, garlic, chilli and ginger and sauté for 2 minutes over a low heat. Stir in the curry powder, then the leek and sauté for 15–20 minutes, stirring occasionally, until the leek is very soft and tender.

Meanwhile, preheat the oven to 190°C/375°C/Gas Mark 5. Wash the salt off the fish under cold running water, then place in a saucepan, skin-side up. Pour in the milk and bring to a simmer, then turn off the heat, cover with a lid and set aside for 5–7 minutes, or until it comes apart in large flakes when pressed. Carefully transfer the fish to a plate, then strain the milk into a jug. When the fish is cool enough to handle, flake the flesh, discarding the skin and bones, and set aside.

Sprinkle the flour into the pan of leeks and stir for 1 minute with a wooden spoon. Pour in half the strained milk, increase to a medium-high heat and continue stirring until you have a very thick sauce. Add the coconut milk a little at a time and keep stirring until the mixture coats the back of the spoon.

6 quails eggs or 3 ordinary eggs, hardboiled and peeled

125–150g (4–5oz) fresh breadcrumbs

1 tbsp olive oil

½ tsp finely ground Sichuan pepper

Add the shrimps to the sauce, giving it a good stir, then add the flaked fish and stir gently over a very low heat for 1 minute. If the sauce seems too thick, add some more of the strained milk. Stir in the coriander and lemon juice and season with black pepper and a little salt if needed.

Half-fill six 200ml (7fl oz) ramekins with the fish mixture. Quarter the quail eggs (or cut the ordinary eggs into eighths) and put 4 pieces in each ramekin. Cover with the remaining fish mixture.

Put the breadcrumbs, olive oil and Sichuan pepper in a bowl, mix well, then sprinkle evenly over the ramekins and place them on a baking sheet. Bake for 8–12 minutes, or until the breadcrumbs are crisp and golden. Serve immediately.

Post Card

CORRESPONDENCE · ADDRESS ONLY

Experimental cook Joanna Harrison moved to England almost a decade ago from Poland, where cooking meat with fruit is second nature. She invented this dish one Friday evening with the ingredients she had to hand – and it was an instant success with her son Adam.

CHICKEN FILLETS
WITH PEACHES IN CORNFLAKES

SERVES 2

2 chicken breast fillets

1 tbsp universal vegetable seasoning, such as Kucharek

2 canned peach halves, thinly sliced

2 tbsp spicy tomato ketchup, such as Dawtona

125g (4oz) cornflakes, finely crushed

1 tbsp sunflower oil for frying

Preheat the oven to 180°C/350°F/Gas Mark 4.

Put the chicken fillets between 2 sheets of cling film and bash them with a meat mallet or small saucepan to flatten to a thickness of roughly 5mm (¼in).

Sprinkle the seasoning on both sides of the chicken, then arrange the peach slices on top, leaving a 1cm (½in) gap at one end of each fillet. Roll the fillet up to enclose the fruit, finishing with the uncovered edge, and secure with a cocktail stick.

Put the ketchup and cornflakes on separate plates. Coat the chicken first in the ketchup, then roll in the cornflakes.

Heat the oil in an ovenproof frying pan or shallow flameproof casserole dish over a low heat and fry the rolls until coloured on the outside and just crisp. Transfer to the oven for 25 minutes, or until cooked through.

Serve with beetroot salad, couscous and potatoes roasted with a little honey.

SPICED LENTIL VEGETABLE CAKES

MAKES 16

200g (7oz) handvo or ondhwa flour (a mixture of ground rice, toor dal and chana dal, available from Indian grocery shops)

500ml (17fl oz) natural yoghurt

about 100ml (3½fl oz) hot water

4 medium carrots, roughly chopped

2 small courgettes, roughly chopped

2 medium potatoes or ½ butternut squash, roughly chopped

2 small onions, roughly chopped

3 handfuls of spinach

4 garlic cloves

2.5cm (1in) piece of fresh ginger, finely chopped

handful of fresh coriander

handful of fresh fenugreek (also known as methi)

2½ tsp red chilli powder

¾ tsp ground turmeric

3 tsp salt

4 tsp sugar

¾ tsp bicarbonate of soda

125g (4oz) coarse semolina

3 tbsp lemon juice (or to taste)

2 tbsp olive oil, plus extra for greasing

3 tbsp mustard seeds

3 tbsp sesame seeds

Put the flour into a large bowl, add the yoghurt and stir in just enough of the hot water to make a thick batter. Cover and leave to stand overnight.

Preheat the oven to 190°C/375°F/Gas Mark 5. Lightly oil a shallow 25 x 25cm (10 x 10in) baking tin.

Place the vegetables, garlic, ginger and fresh herbs in a food processor and whiz to a coarse paste.

Discard any excess water from the flour mixture, then add to the processed vegetables, along with the spices, salt, sugar, bicarbonate of soda, semolina and lemon juice. Whiz again to combine.

Put half the oil in a small saucepan and place on a medium heat. When hot, add half the mustard and sesame seeds, and wait until they pop. Add them to the vegetable mixture and stir well. Pour into the prepared baking tin and spread evenly.

Heat the remaining oil and cook the remaining mustard and sesame seeds as before, then pour them evenly over the vegetable mixture. Place in the oven for 45–60 minutes, until a golden crust has formed on the surface. (Ovens vary, so if it's not brown enough, bake for another 10–15 minutes.) Set aside to cool in the tin, then cut into squares and serve warm.

Vegetarian Dr Amit Mehta has inherited his passion for food from his mum, who gave him the family recipe for this classic Gujarati dish. It's delicious eaten hot or cold, but he prefers it freshly baked, straight from the oven.

Rachel Kelly's father, Henry, learned to make this dish when he was in the army in Malaya in the 1950s, and one of her earliest memories is of him cooking it at home. When she grew up Rachel started making curries of her own, using everything her father had taught her as a girl, and this curry uses her own spice blend including the Malaysian 'holy quartet' of ingredients: fennel, cinnamon, cloves and cardamom.

HENRY'S MALAY JUNGLE CURRY

SERVES 4–6

2 tbsp vegetable oil

1 tsp ground coriander

1 tsp ground cumin

1 tsp chilli powder (or to taste)

3 medium onions, halved and sliced from root to tip

salt

4–5 garlic cloves, very finely chopped

1 tsp finely grated fresh ginger

12 chicken thighs, on the bone

1 tbsp tomato purée

2 litres (3½ pints) chicken or vegetable stock

2–3 large baking potatoes, quartered

1 tsp tamarind paste (optional)

400ml can of coconut milk

8 eggs, hardboiled and peeled

First make the curry powder. Put the seeds, peppercorns, cinnamon stick and chillies into a hot dry frying pan and fry for 2–3 minutes, shaking them occasionally, until fragrant. Allow to cool slightly, then grind finely (preferably in a spice grinder). Add all the ground spices, and grind again so that the mixture is well combined. Store in a tightly sealed jar. The powder will stay fresh for about 2 months without losing any of its fabulous aromas.

To make the curry, heat the oil in a large, heavy-based saucepan over a medium heat. Add the ground coriander, cumin and chilli powder, plus 2 tablespoons of the Malay curry powder. Stir thoroughly in the oil, then add the onions, stir again and sprinkle with a little salt. Cover with a lid and cook for 10 minutes, stirring occasionally, until the onions are beginning to soften.

Stir in the garlic and ginger, and cook for another 2 minutes. Now add the chicken thighs, mix well and cook for 5 minutes, until the meat is beginning to colour.

Add the tomato purée and at least half the stock – it should cover the chicken. Bring to the boil, then cover and simmer on the lowest heat for 45 minutes.

For the Malay curry powder

2 tbsp coriander seeds

2 tbsp cumin seeds

seeds from 1 tbsp green cardamom pods

2 tsp fennel seeds

1 tbsp yellow mustard seeds

1 tbsp black peppercorns

5cm (2in) cinnamon stick, crushed

2-3 large dried chillies, roughly chopped

2½ tbsp ground turmeric

1 tsp ground ginger

1 tsp ground nutmeg

½ tsp ground cloves

Meanwhile, put the potatoes in a pan of cold water, bring to the boil and parboil for 5 minutes. Drain, add the potatoes to the curry and cook for a further 20 minutes. You might need to add more stock. At this point, I like to add tamarind paste to sharpen up the flavours and give the curry a fresh taste, but this is optional.

When the potatoes are cooked, add the coconut milk and cook over a medium heat for 10 minutes. Taste and adjust the seasoning, then add the hardboiled eggs, cut into wedges if liked, and continue cooking just long enough for the eggs to heat through.

Serve the curry with plain steamed rice, cucumber raita and small bowls of salted peanuts, chopped tomatoes, spring onion and pineapple for everyone to help themselves.

VINTAGE LAVENDER & LEMON BLANCMANGE

SERVES 4–6

sunflower oil for greasing

65g (2½oz) cornflour

600ml (1 pint) full-fat milk

fine zest from 1 large or 2 small lemons

2 tsp clear honey

1 tbsp rose water

3–5 drops natural yellow food colouring (depending on depth of colour wanted)

For the lavender sugar

500g (1lb) caster sugar

1½–3 tbsp culinary grade lavender husks

First make the lavender sugar. Combine the sugar and lavender husks in an airtight container and leave for up to a week to allow the sugar to become infused with lavender. This quantity of lavender sugar will last a very long time and make quite a number of blancmanges.

Lightly oil a 900ml (1½ pint) blancmange mould and place it upside down on a sheet of kitchen paper.

Sift the cornflour into a bowl. Add 125ml (4fl oz) of the milk and stir until smooth. Set aside.

Pour the remaining milk into a saucepan, add the lemon zest, 4 tablespoons of lavender sugar with the husks sifted out, the honey, rose water and food colouring. Heat the mixture until it reaches boiling point, stirring continuously to prevent it from catching.

Take the pan off the heat and quickly stir in the cornflour liquid. Place the pan back on a low heat and stir constantly for 3–5 minutes, until the mixture thickens and forms ribbons on the surface when you lift the spoon. If it begins to catch while you're stirring, take the pan off the heat, continuing to stir, and return it to the heat after 30 seconds. Don't be tempted to beat the mixture as this will introduce air bubbles and your blancmange will have a pitted surface where the air bubbles have burst. The mixture needs to be smooth and thick in order to ensure that the surface of your blancmange is blemish-free.

Pour the mixture into the prepared mould and set aside to cool. When lukewarm, place in the fridge for 4–5 hours, until firm.

To turn out the blancmange, place the mould in a bowl of hot water for 20–30 seconds, taking care not to get the contents wet. Remove from the water, dry the outside of the mould, then place a plate on top. Invert both plate and mould and the blancmange will slide out, making a suction noise when you lift off the mould.

Emma Muscat makes this delicately fragranced blancmange using her great great grandmother's Wedgewood mould. She developed this recipe recently using Mrs Beeton's cookbook for inspiration. Be sure to use rosewater and not the more expensive rose essence, which will overwhelm this dish.

APPLOFFI PIE

SERVES 6–8

400–600g (13oz–1lb 2oz) condensed milk (I use the full 600g/1lb 2oz but you can use less: it's down to personal taste)

1 large Bramley apple, peeled, cored and sliced

2 Cox's apples, peeled, cored and sliced

50ml (2fl oz) orange juice

50g (2oz) light muscovado sugar

425ml (14½fl oz) double cream

25g (1oz) caster sugar

½ tsp ground cinnamon

freshly grated nutmeg

For the pastry
250g (8oz) plain flour, plus extra for dusting

25g (1oz) icing sugar

125g (4oz) cold butter, cubed

1 egg plus 1 egg yolk

Preheat the oven to 140°C/275°F/Gas Mark 1.

Put the unopened cans of condensed milk into an ovenproof casserole (it's worth doing as many cans as will fit to save energy and then storing them to use at a later date). Cover the cans with water and bring to the boil on the hob. Cover with a lid and transfer to the oven for 3½ hours. Remove the cans from the water and set aside to cool.

To make the pastry, put the flour and sugar into a bowl, add the butter and rub together until the mixture resembles breadcrumbs. Work in the egg and yolk to form a dough, then wrap in cling film and chill for 30 minutes.

Preheat the oven to 180°C/350°F/Gas Mark 4.

On a lightly floured work surface, roll out the pastry to the thickness of a £1 coin and use to line a 23cm (9in) loose-bottomed flan tin. Prick the base with a fork, then line the pastry case with crumpled greaseproof paper. Fill with ceramic baking beans, dried pulses or rice and bake for 15–20 minutes. Remove the paper and beans, then return the pastry case to the oven for a further 5 minutes, until it is evenly golden. Set aside to cool.

To make the filling, put the apples, orange juice and muscovado sugar in a saucepan and heat gently until the fruit is pulpy and quite dry. Set aside until completely cold.

To assemble the pie, open the tins of condensed milk and empty the toffee into the pastry case, spreading it out evenly. Spread the apple on top of this. Whip the cream with the caster sugar and cinnamon until it forms soft peaks, then spread this over the apple. Sprinkle a little nutmeg over the cream and serve.

Sisters Margaret Hayes and Kathrine Norris remember helping their mother to prepare these puddings when they were children, with help from sisters Jenny and Lynette and brother Roger. Margaret and Kathrine are passionate about baking, and have adapted their grandmother's recipe so that it is gluten free.

MUMMY'S YUMMY GLUTEN-FREE CHRISTMAS PUDDING

SERVES 6–8

200ml (7fl oz) sunflower oil, plus extra for greasing

150g (5oz) dark brown sugar

4 eggs

300ml (½ pint) orange juice

275g (9oz) currants

275g (9oz) sultanas

275g (9oz) raisins

½ tsp salt

½ tsp ground cinnamon

2 tsp ground mixed spices

1 tsp ground nutmeg

100g (3½oz) gluten-free self-raising flour

200g (7oz) gluten-free breadcrumbs (we blitz our own from Yes! You Can gluten-free bread)

Grease a 1.2 litre (2 pint) pudding basin with sunflower oil. Cut circles of greaseproof paper and muslin large enough to cover the basin with at least 8cm (3in) overhang.

Put all the ingredients except the flour and breadcrumbs in a mixing bowl and set aside to soak for 4 hours.

Stir the flour and breadcrumbs into the soaked mixture and make a wish. Spoon into the prepared basin, cover with the greaseproof and muslin circles, and tie securely with kitchen string.

Place a trivet or old jam jar lid in a large saucepan, sit the pudding on it, then pour in enough boiling water to come halfway up the side of the basin. Cover and simmer for 9 hours, checking regularly and topping up the water if necessary.

Serve straight away with cream, or cover with fresh greaseproof and foil or store in a dry place for up to 6 months. Enjoy this pudding at any celebration.

Clare Rubicondo's youngest son started calling her 'Mummy Pie' because she is his mummy and she makes pies – and this is how her strawberry and cream cheese pie is know in her family. It is the first pie she has made with gluten-free pastry, and combines all the ingredients that she loves. This pie will bring a smile to your face when you take your first bite!

MUMMY PIE

SERVES 8–12

250g (8oz) gluten-free plain flour, plus extra for dusting

pinch of salt

1 tsp xanthan gum

1 tbsp caster sugar

50g (2oz) unsalted butter, cubed, plus extra for greasing

50g (2oz) vegetable fat

1 egg, chilled

½ tsp vanilla extract

1 egg, beaten, to glaze

For the cream cheese filling
300g (10oz) cream cheese

2 tbsp icing sugar

2 tbsp whipping cream

zest of ½ lemon

Preheat the oven to 160°C/325°F/Gas Mark 3. Grease and flour a deep pie dish (about 1.8 litres/3 pints in capacity).

To make the pastry, sift the flour, salt, xanthan gum and sugar into a bowl. Add the butter and vegetable fat and rub together or process until the mixture resembles breadcrumbs.

Put the egg and vanilla extract in a small bowl and mix lightly with a fork until the yolk breaks. Pour into the flour mixture and stir or process on a low setting until a dough starts to form, adding 1–2 tablespoons cold water to the dough mixture if it seems too dry. Wrap the dough in cling film and refrigerate for 30 minutes.

On a lightly floured work surface, roll out the pastry to a thickness of about 5mm (¼in) and use it to line the prepared dish. Chill in the fridge for 10 minutes.

Prick the base of the chilled pastry case with a fork and lightly brush egg wash around the sides and bottom. Bake in the centre of the oven for 15 minutes, or until golden. Set aside to cool.

Meanwhile, put the cream cheese, icing sugar, whipping cream and lemon zest in a bowl and mix together. Spread over the

For the strawberry filling
400g (13oz) ripe strawberries, hulled and chopped
4 tbsp caster sugar
3 tbsp cornflour
250ml (8fl oz) water

For the topping
600ml (1 pint) whipping cream
2 tbsp icing sugar
1 chocolate flake, crumbled

bottom and up the sides of the cooled pastry case, then refrigerate until needed.

To make the strawberry filling, place the berries in a saucepan. Mix the sugar and cornflour in a small bowl, then pour over the strawberries and mix with a long-handled spoon. Add the water and bring to the boil, stirring constantly. Reduce to a simmer and allow to thicken, still stirring – this will take about 7 minutes. Remove from the heat and set aside to cool. When cold, spread it over the cream cheese layer.

To make the topping, put the cream and icing sugar into a bowl and lightly whip to soft peaks. Pipe or spoon it on top of the pie, then sprinkle generously with the crumbled chocolate and refrigerate until ready to serve.

Laura Wiles was given this foolproof family recipe by her mum when she moved into her own flat and started cooking for herself. Since then Laura has adapted it to have more of a kick, and it always receives rave reviews when she bakes it for her work colleagues.

LAURA'S FIERY GINGER CAKE

SERVES 6-8

250g (8oz) self-raising flour

1 tsp bicarbonate of soda

1 tbsp black pepper

1 tbsp ground ginger

1 tsp ground cinnamon

1 tsp ground mixed spice

125g (4oz) butter, cubed, plus extra for greasing

75g (3oz) stem ginger, grated (freezing it makes grating easier)

125g (4oz) dark muscovado sugar

2 tbsp black treacle

2 tbsp golden syrup

250ml (8fl oz) milk

1 large egg

For the topping
50g (2oz) icing sugar, sifted

1 tbsp lemon juice

3 pieces of crystallised stem ginger, grated

Preheat the oven to 180°C/350°F/Gas Mark 4. Butter a 1kg (2lb) loaf tin or line it with greaseproof paper.

Sift the flour, bicarbonate of soda, pepper and ground spices into a bowl. Add the butter and rub in with your fingertips until the mixture resembles breadcrumbs. Add the stem ginger and set aside.

Put the sugar, treacle and syrup into a saucepan and heat until the sugar has dissolved. Add the milk and stir gently until it reaches just below the boil. Make a well in the flour mixture and pour in the hot milk, stirring constantly with a wooden spoon. Add the egg and mix well. The mixture will resemble a thick liquid. Pour it into the prepared loaf tin and bake for 50–60 minutes. The cake is ready when a knife inserted into the middle comes out clean. Set aside to cool in the tin. Turn out only when cold.

To make the topping, put the icing sugar and lemon juice in a bowl and mix until smooth. Drizzle the mixture over the cake, then sprinkle the crystallised stem ginger on top. Serve hot or cold.

LAVENDER & ORANGE CAKE

SERVES 12

100ml (3½fl oz) full-fat milk

4–6 tbsp culinary lavender

4 eggs

450g (14½oz) wholemeal flour, plus extra for dusting

1 tbsp baking powder

450g (14½oz) caster sugar

450g (14½oz) butter, plus extra for greasing

¼ tsp vanilla extract

For the icing
115g (3¾oz) butter

325g (11oz) icing sugar

2½ tbsp orange juice

½ tsp vanilla extract

2 tsp grated orange zest

For the icing flowers (optional)
250g (8oz) royal icing sugar, plus extra for dusting

1 tsp water

3 drops of purple food colouring gel

19g tube of ready-made purple writing icing

The day before you want to make the cake, combine the milk and lavender in a cup, cover with cling film and refrigerate overnight.

Preheat the oven to 200°C/400°F/Gas Mark 6. Butter and flour three 18cm (7in) loose-bottomed sponge tins.

Place the lavender-infused milk in a small saucepan over a low heat until a strong lavender fragrance is released and the milk is a dark lavender colour. Set aside to cool.

Put the eggs in a bowl and whisk until fluffy. Add the flour and baking powder and mix well.

Put the sugar and butter in a separate bowl and beat together until light and fluffy. Add to the flour mixture and beat again until light and fluffy. Stir in the vanilla extract.

Strain the lavender buds out of the milk and add the liquid to the batter. Mix thoroughly until smooth. (This is best done with a food mixer – 30 seconds on a slow speed, then 90 seconds on a high speed.) Divide the mixture equally between the prepared tins and bake for 35 minutes, until well risen, slightly golden and springy to touch. Cool in the tins for 10 minutes, then turn out on to wire racks to cool.

To make the icing, put the butter in a bowl and beat until smooth. Add the icing sugar a bit at time, beating well between each addition, until light and fluffy. Beat in the orange juice until evenly combined, then stir in the vanilla extract and orange zest.

Take 2 of the cooled cakes and spread a quarter of the icing on each one. Sandwich the 3 layers together. Spread the remainder of the icing over the top and sides of the whole cake.

To make the icing flowers, put the sugar in a bowl, add the water and mix with a wooden spoon or a food mixer fitted with a dough hook until it reaches a dough-like consistency. Gather into a ball, place on a work surface lightly dusted with icing sugar and knead for 2–3 minutes, until very smooth and slightly glossy. Knead in the purple gel until the colour is evenly distributed. Roll out the icing to a thickness of 5mm (¼in), then use different sizes of flower-shaped cutters to stamp out as many flowers as desired. Press them on to the surface of the iced cake, using a dab of the writing icing to help them stick.

Tiffany Hall's baking inspiration comes from her father, who used to bake cakes for family and friends, but passed away when Tiffany was a little girl. When she was 13 Tiffany decided to start baking in his memory, and has never looked back. She invented this recipe when her mother brought back fresh lavender from a holiday.

Samantha Hope's boyfriend suffers from coeliac disease, which means he can't eat any wheat or gluten. She developed this recipe as a sort of rock cake, but unlike the traditional version these little boulders are soft, light and totally gluten free. They are also the best cakes Samantha's boyfriend has ever tasted!

CHOC, FUDGE & COCONUT BOULDERS

MAKES 14

200g (7oz) gluten-free plain flour

2 tsp gluten-free baking powder

100g (3½oz) margarine or butter

100g (3½oz) golden caster sugar

70g (2¾oz) dark chocolate chips

70g (2¾oz) fudge, broken into pieces

85g (3¼oz) desiccated coconut

1 tsp vanilla extract

1 large egg, beaten

milk (optional)

Preheat oven to 200°C/400°F/Gas Mark 6. Line 2 baking sheets with baking parchment.

Place the flour and baking powder in a bowl and rub in the margarine or butter until the mixture resembles breadcrumbs. Add the sugar, chocolate chips, fudge pieces and coconut and stir well.

Combine the vanilla extract and beaten egg. Add to the dry ingredients and mix lightly with a fork until the mixture starts to come together. It should be crumbly and hold together in your hands, but if it's too dry, add a drop of milk.

Place 7 small mounds, about the size of a heaped dessertspoon, on each baking sheet, spacing them well apart, and press the top of each with the back of a fork to create rough edges.

Bake for 15–20 minutes, or until golden. Cool on a wire rack and serve warm or cold. If stored in an airtight container, the boulders will keep for 5–6 days.

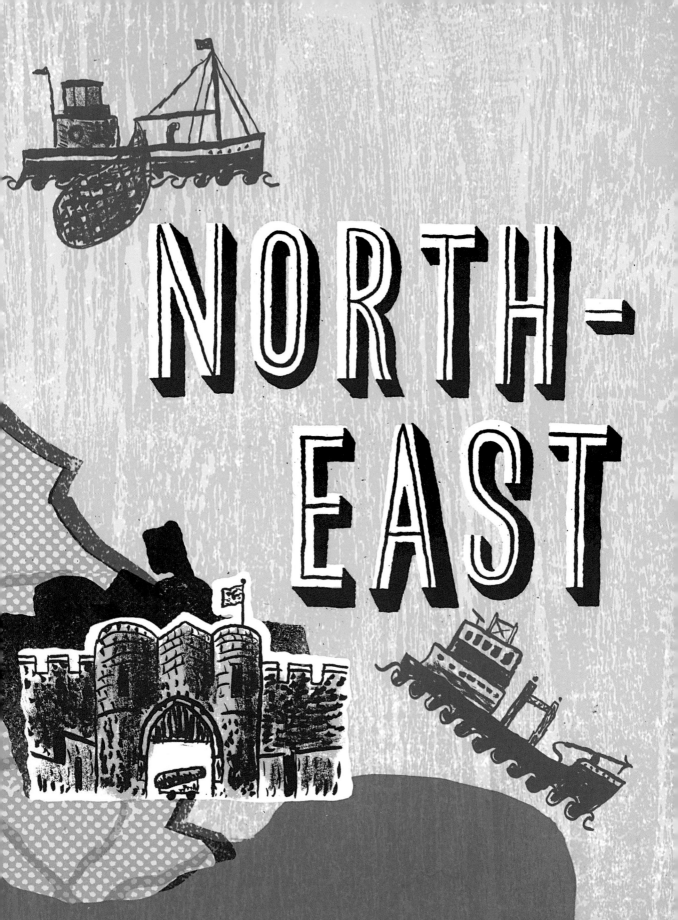

NORTH-
EAST

Salted Caramel Bourbon Syrup

NORTH-EAST

The venue for the North-East heat was the Great Yorkshire Showground on the second day of the Harrogate Autumn Flower Show, a massively popular event that attracts around 35,000 visitors each year. Joining the judges for both this and the North-West heat was Andi Oliver, who thoroughly enjoyed the great selection of spicy dishes on offer!

Curry, in all its deliciously spicy guises, took centre stage for this heat: Fragrant White Chicken Korma, Thai Green Goddess Curry, Aloo Keema and, rather alarmingly, one dish billed as The World's Hottest Curry! As you'd expect from this region, there were some great Yorkshire Puddings, among them an innovative recipe that served Yorkshire puds with duck and hoisin sauce – definitely not your standard Sunday roast accompaniment. Other more traditional offerings from the region included Penistone Pork Pie, Chicken & Bacon Parcels and Smoky Bacon, Onion & Cheese Scones.

There were also some unusual and delectable sweet treats, such as an elaborate Baked Trifle, Great Auntie Madge's Carrot Cake and a delicious cake made with nettles and bramble jelly. But perhaps the most appropriate for the day was the cheery-sounding Taste of Sunshine cake – a slice of which was just what everyone needed as the rain came pouring down. *Food Glorious Food* had been blessed with sunny weather throughout but our luck ran out at this heat. Fortunately the rain arrived near the end of day when most contestants were safely in the shelter of the judges' tent waiting to hear the results.

Jacqueline Marsden is a pork pie producer, and she sells her Penistone Pies at Holmfirth and Penistone markets. This recipe is her granddad Freddie's, who was the village butcher for over 40 years. Jacqueline still uses his Little Champion pie-making machine and locally sourced ingredients.

PENISTONE PORK PIE

MAKES A 500G (1LB) PORK PIE

175g (6oz) belly of pork, minced or chopped

175g (6oz) shoulder of pork, minced or chopped

1 tbsp fresh white breadcrumbs

½ tsp salt

1½ tsp white pepper

pinch of freshly grated nutmeg

2 twists of freshly ground black pepper

1 egg, beaten, to glaze

½ sachet of powdered gelatine

For the pastry
190g (6½oz) plain flour

¼ tsp baking powder

¼ tsp salt

65g (2½oz) vegetable fat, plus extra for greasing

60ml (2½fl oz) water

2 tsp semi-skimmed milk

Preheat the oven to 200°C/400°F/Gas Mark 6.

Place both lots of pork in a bowl with the breadcrumbs and all the seasoning. Mix well.

To make the pastry, sift the flour, baking powder and salt into a bowl. Melt the vegetable fat in a saucepan, add the water and milk and bring to the boil. Quickly mix this liquid into the flour to form a dough.

Warm a 500g (1lb) pork pie tin in the oven for just a few seconds, then grease lightly. Take two-thirds of the warm pastry, place it in the tin and use your fingers to press it over the bottom and up the sides. If the pastry is not warm enough to mould, microwave it for just a few seconds.

Spoon the meat filling into the pastry case until it is 5mm (¼in) below the top edge. Roll out the remaining pastry to make a lid, place it on top of the pie and crimp the edges firmly together. Reroll any pastry offcuts and use a decorative cutter to stamp out a shape for the top of the pie (I use a pig-shaped cutter). Stab the top of the pie with a skewer or chopstick to make a small steam hole, then glaze with the beaten egg and bake for 10 minutes. Lower the heat to 180°C/350°F/Gas Mark 4 and bake for a further 50 minutes. The pie is ready when the pastry is golden brown and a temperature probe inserted in the middle registers 180–190°C (350–375°F). Set aside to cool to room temperature.

Using a fine skewer, make a hole in the pie, ensuring it goes right through the meat. Make up the gelatine according to the packet instructions, then spoon it into the hole gradually, giving it time to percolate through the meat. You will have slightly more gelatine than you need.

Set the pie aside until completely cold, then turn out of the tin, cut into wedges and serve.

Using Tuscan cooking methods learned from her father and wild game from her farm in Wensleydale, Yara Gremoli has created her own take on the traditional lasagne. Yara moved to England over a decade ago and feels that this lasagne combines the best of her Tuscan roots with delicious local Yorkshire produce.

YARA'S GAME LASAGNE

SERVES 8

600g (1lb 2oz) mixed game (e.g. venison, hare, pigeon, wild duck), cleaned, trimmed of all fat and sinew and finely diced

6 tbsp extra virgin olive oil

2 garlic cloves, crushed

sprig of thyme

2 tbsp balsamic vinegar

1 onion, finely chopped

2 carrots, finely chopped

1 celery stick, finely chopped

Place the meat in a non-metallic bowl. Add 1 tablespoon of the olive oil, a clove of garlic, the thyme and balsamic vinegar and mix well. Cover and leave in the fridge to marinate overnight.

Put 4 tablespoons of the olive oil in a frying pan with the onion, carrots, celery, mushrooms (if using), chilli and remaining garlic. Cover and cook over a low heat for 15–20 minutes, stirring occasionally, until the contents have softened. Once the vegetables start sticking to the bottom of the pan, set aside.

Remove the garlic and thyme from the marinated meat and discard. In another pan, heat the remaining tablespoon of oil over a high heat add the meat and marinade and cook, covered, for 30–60 seconds. The game usually releases water, so drain off all

150g (5oz) field mushrooms, finely sliced (optional)

2 dried red bird's eye chillies (or to taste), broken in half

125ml (4fl oz) red wine

2 x 400g cans of peeled plum tomatoes

2 vegetable stock cubes

1 tsp sugar

125g (4oz) pecorino semistagionato or crumbly Swaledale cheese, grated

For the pasta
425g (14oz) '00' flour

salt

4 eggs

1 tbsp water

semolina flour

2 tbsp vegetable oil for cooking

For the béchamel sauce
75g (3oz) butter, plus extra for greasing

75g (3oz) plain flour

750ml (1¼ pints) milk

¼ tsp ground nutmeg

the liquid as often as necessary (this will take the gamey edge off a little) until the meat is very dry and starts sticking to the pan. Stir and season to taste, then add the cooked vegetables and wine and stir again. Now add the tomatoes and crumble in the stock cubes, lower the heat and stir well until the cubes have dissolved. Cover and leave to simmer for 2 hours, stirring occasionally. The sauce should be neither too stiff nor too runny, so adjust the consistency as necessary, either by adding water or by cooking uncovered for a little longer.

Meanwhile, make the pasta. Sift the flour and a pinch of salt into a large bowl. Make a well in the middle and add the eggs, gradually mixing them into the flour with your fingertips until a dough forms. Add a little water if the dough is too firm, or a little semolina flour if too soft. On a work surface lightly dusted with semolina flour (if necessary), knead the dough for a few minutes until smooth and elastic. Shape the dough into a ball, wrap in cling film and place in the fridge for 20 minutes.

To make the béchamel sauce, melt the butter in a saucepan over low heat. Take off the heat and stir in the flour a little at a time until you have a thick paste. Gradually add the milk, stirring to incorporate each addition before adding the next. Add a pinch of salt and the nutmeg, then place over a medium heat and bring to the boil, stirring constantly. Lower the heat and stir for 5 minutes, then set aside to cool, stirring occasionally.

Preheat the oven to 180°C/350°F/Gas Mark 4. Lightly butter eight 200ml (7fl oz) ramekins.

Dust a work surface with semolina flour and roll out the pasta dough as thinly as possible. Using a pastry cutter or one of your ramekins, stamp out 24 circles of pasta.

Spoon a layer of the game sauce, about 1cm (½in) deep, into each ramekin. Place a disc of pasta over the sauce in each ramekin. Spoon another layer of game sauce on top, then cover with béchamel. Repeat these layers (pasta, meat sauce, béchamel) at least twice more, finishing with plenty of béchamel.

Sprinkle the pecorino on top of the dishes and place in the oven for 20 minutes, or until the cheese has browned. Leave to rest for a few minutes before serving.

YARA'S GAME LASAGNE

Pig farmer Tori Swiers set up the North Yorkshire branch of Ladies in Pigs, a group dedicated to promoting British pork and bacon. This is a recipe she regularly cooks with meat from her own pigs, and although the dish uses store-cupboard ingredients and is simple to prepare, it must be made with British pork.

PEPPERED PORK

SERVES 4–6

875g (1¾lb) pork fillet, trimmed of excess fat

salt and freshly ground black pepper

1 tsp butter

1 tsp vegetable oil

285ml (9½fl oz) white wine or sherry

1 tsp redcurrant jelly

285ml (9½fl oz) double cream

Cut the meat into 4cm (1¾in) slices. Place between 2 sheets of cling film, spacing them well apart, and flatten to a thickness of 5mm (¼in) by bashing them with a rolling pin or small saucepan. Take care not to hit too hard as you must avoid tearing the meat. Season to taste with salt and plenty of freshly ground pepper.

Heat the butter and oil in a frying pan over a high heat, then add the pork slices a few at a time, ensuring they don't touch or overlap. Fry for 5 minutes, turning regularly, until cooked through and brown on both sides. Do not overcook or the meat will toughen. Transfer to a warm plate, cover loosely with foil and keep warm.

When all the slices are cooked, add the wine to the pan and bubble over a high heat for 6–8 minutes, or until the liquid has reduced by two-thirds. Add more pepper and the redcurrant jelly, and stir until the jelly has dissolved.

Take the pan off the heat and whisk in the cream (this ought to prevent it from splitting). Return to the heat and warm through.

Serve the pork slices on warm plates with the sauce spooned over them, and offer new potatoes and a selection of fresh vegetables to go with them.

RAHILA'S FRAGRANT WHITE CHICKEN KORMA

SERVES 6–8

3 tbsp vegetable oil

25g (1oz) butter (optional)

1 tsp coriander seeds, freshly ground

1 tsp cumin seeds, freshly ground

2 medium onions, finely chopped

1 heaped tbsp minced garlic

1 heaped tbsp finely grated ginger

1–2½ tsp salt

1–2 tsp ground white pepper

1 green chilli, finely ground

1kg (2lb) chicken thighs, boned, skinned, trimmed of all fat and sinew, and chopped into 2.5cm (1in) dice

1–2 tbsp finely grated fresh coconut or desiccated coconut

1–1½ tbsp finely ground pistachio nuts

1–1½ tbsp finely ground almonds

1–1½ tbsp finely ground cashew nuts

3 green chillies, halved lengthways, 1 of the chillies deseeded

250–500ml (8–17fl oz) water

300g (10oz) natural yoghurt, lightly whisked

freshly ground seeds from 14–16 cardamom pods

coriander, freshly chopped, for garnish

Heat the oil and butter (if using) in a pan, add the ground coriander and cumin and fry for 30 seconds, or until the colour changes slightly. Add the onions and fry until soft and slightly golden. Add the garlic and ginger and fry for 2 minutes over a low heat. Stir in the salt and pepper to taste, then add the ground green chilli and cook for 30 seconds.

Add the chicken, increase the heat and stir-fry for 15–20 minutes, or until the oil separates from the meat. Do not allow the meat to brown.

Add the coconut, pistachios, almonds, cashews, halved chillies and the water – you need enough water to nearly cover the other ingredients. Bring to the boil, then simmer for 5 minutes. Then stir in the yoghurt and ground cardamom and simmer for 20 minutes, or until the oil separates.

Garnish with the chopped coriander and serve with plain boiled rice, roti or naan.

Passionate about Pakistani food, Rahila Hussain learnt everything she knows about cooking from her late mother and travels to Pakistan regularly to collect recipes and get new ideas for dishes. This healthy version of chicken korma uses natural yoghurt instead of cream – and Rahila also omits the turmeric, which is why her dish isn't yellow.

Christopher Blackburn is the winner of the 2011 and 2012 Yorkshire Pudding Challenge, and also a huge fan of Chinese food, so he decided to experiment with the two. This dish is his perfect combination of British and Chinese cuisines, and the secret ingredient is the beef dripping.

CHINESE-STYLE YORKSHIRE PUDDINGS
WITH DUCK & HOISIN SAUCE

MAKES 12

12 tsp beef dripping (1 tsp for each muffin tin cup)

225g (7½oz) plain flour

4 eggs

300ml (½ pint) milk

1 tsp salt

1 tsp Chinese five- spice powder

For the filling
1 duck leg

cucumber, cut into matchsticks

spring onion, shredded into matchstick lengths

For the hoisin sauce
1 tbsp Chinese five-spice powder

¼ tbsp Tabasco sauce

1 tbsp rice wine vinegar

½ tbsp sesame oil

3 tbsp dark soy sauce

1 tbsp tomato purée

1 tbsp honey

First prepare the meat for the filling. Place the duck leg in a steamer, cover and steam for 2 hours. Pat dry with kitchen paper.

Preheat the oven to 180°C/350°F/Gas Mark 4. Meanwhile, mix together all the sauce ingredients. Put the cooked duck leg in a roasting tin, pour half the sauce over it and roast for 20 minutes. Set aside to cool.

Increase the oven temperature to its highest setting. Take a 12-hole muffin tin and divide the dripping between the cups. Place in the oven until sizzling hot.

Put the flour, eggs, milk, salt and five spice powder in a bowl and mix well. Pour the batter into the hot dripping and place in the oven, reducing the temperature to 220°C/425°F/Gas Mark 7. Bake for 20 minutes, or until well risen and golden.

Place the remaining hoisin sauce in a double boiler and heat gently.

Pat the duck leg dry, then use 2 forks to shred the meat from the bone. Combine with the hot sauce.

Put some of the duck mixture into each Yorkshire pudding. Arrange 2 neat rows of the cucumber and spring onions on a wooden board or serving platter and sit the filled Yorkies on top. Encourage people to help themselves and sprinkle some of the cucumber and spring onion on top of the duck.

Primary school teacher Misbah Parveen was born in Pakistan, and grew up on this dish, which her mother used to make. She now cooks this healthier version once a week for her own family, served with warm chapatis, and last time her mother visited she declared it was better than the original recipe.

MISBAH'S ALOO KEEMA

SERVES 4

3–4 tbsp olive oil

1 tbsp butter (optional)

2 medium onions, thinly sliced

salt

1.5cm (¾in) piece of fresh ginger, chopped

8 garlic cloves, chopped

7–8 green chillies, chopped

400g can of chopped tomatoes

750ml (1¼ pints) water

1kg (2lb) minced lamb or mutton

8 new potatoes, scrubbed and halved

1 tsp garam masala

handful of coriander, chopped

Heat the oil with the butter (if using) in a saucepan. Add the onions and salt to taste. Fry until the onions are slightly brown. Add the ginger, garlic and chillies and fry for 5 minutes.

Pour in the tomatoes and 250ml (8fl oz) of the water, and cook over a medium heat until the liquid evaporates, the ingredients turn into a paste, and separated oil can be seen.

Add the mince and fry until it changes colour. Add another 250ml (8fl oz) of the water and cook slowly until it evaporates. Turn up the heat and cook briskly for 7 minutes. Add the potatoes and cook for a further 5 minutes. Add the remaining water and cook over a low heat for 15 minutes, or until the potatoes are ready (you might need to add a little more water). Let the water evaporate, then cook for 5 minutes.

Sprinkle with the garam masala and chopped coriander, and serve with naan bread, pitta bread or chapattis.

Mother-of-five Jacqui Campbell Martin learnt to cook from her own mother, who used to make everything from scratch. Jacqui regularly prepares this dish for family and friends, making a whole day of preparing the ingredients with help from the kids. For a quick version you could use dried squid-ink pasta and fresh crab meat instead.

SQUID INK PASTA
WITH CRAB

SERVES 4-6

2 medium-sized live brown crabs

olive oil

3 banana shallots, chopped

3 garlic cloves, chopped

pinch of dried chilli flakes

3 very ripe medium tomatoes, skinned, deseeded and chopped

generous splash of white wine

handful of parsley, chopped

To prepare the crabs, place them in the freezer for 15–30 minutes to send them to sleep. Meanwhile, bring a large pan of water to the boil.

Cook the crabs in the boiling water for about 30 minutes, then transfer to a bowl of iced water. When cool enough to handle, pick the meat from the shells, keeping the brown and white meat separate.

To make the pasta, place the eggs and ink in a food processor with a blade attachment and whiz for a few seconds. Add the flour, salt and pepper along with a splash of olive oil and whiz again until a ball of dough forms. Alternatively, to make the pasta by hand, place the flour in a bowl, make a well in the centre and add the

For the pasta

4 eggs

1 tbsp squid ink (about 4 sachets)

**400g (14oz) plain or '00' flour,
plus a little extra for dusting**

**salt and freshly ground black
pepper**

olive oil

semolina for dusting

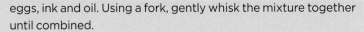

eggs, ink and oil. Using a fork, gently whisk the mixture together until combined.

Lightly flour a work surface and knead the dough for about 10 minutes, adding a little extra flour if it still feels a bit sticky. Wrap in cling film and chill for at least 30 minutes.

Roll out the dough as thinly as possible on a work surface lightly dusted with semolina, or pass it several times through a pasta machine, starting on the widest setting and gradually working down to the finest. Dust with a little semolina if it becomes sticky.

Cut the pasta into your preferred shape – I like tagliatelle – and set aside to dry. It will be ready to cook in about 15 minutes.

Meanwhile, boil another pan of water for it, adding some salt and a little olive oil.

To make the sauce, heat a little olive oil in a large pan. Add the shallots and garlic and sweat until translucent. Add the chilli flakes and tomatoes, cook for 5–6 minutes, until they start to break down, then add the wine. Cook for a further 2–3 minutes, until everything is soft, then set aside.

Take the brown crab meat and either mash it with a fork or use a hand blender to whiz it into a smooth paste. Add this, along with the white crab meat, to the prepared sauce. Season to taste.

Cook the pasta in the boiling water for 3–4 minutes, or until al dente. Reserve a few ladles of the cooking water in a jug, then drain the pasta and add to the sauce. Add the parsley and mix thoroughly, adding some of the reserved cooking water if the mixture looks a bit dry.

Serve the pasta, garnished with Parmesan and lemon wedges if you wish, in a large bowl in the middle of the table and let everyone help themselves.

SQUID INK PASTA WITH CRAB

Experimental baker Lewis Allsopp had a raspberry toastie in a restaurant and decided to try making his own version with strawberries and chocolate. After a few attempts he's hit upon the perfect combination, and it's become a family classic and a favourite amongst his friends.

CHOCOLATE & STRAWBERRY SANDWICH

SERVES 1

2 medium strawberries, cut into 5mm (¼in) slices

2 slices of brioche, 2.5cm (1in) thick

35g (1¼oz) milk chocolate, 20g (¾oz) roughly chopped, the rest grated

25ml (1fl oz) whipping cream

1 tsp icing sugar

1 sprig of mint

Preheat a toastie-maker.

Place half the strawberries on 1 slice of brioche and sprinkle with the chopped chocolate. Top with the second slice of brioche. Place in the hot toastie-maker for 2–3 minutes, until the bread is golden brown and the chocolate has melted.

Meanwhile, whip the cream until light and fluffy and spoon into a piping bag.

Cut the toasted sandwich into diagonal slices and place on a plate. Sift the icing sugar over the sandwich and sprinkle with the grated chocolate.

Pipe the whipped cream on to a corner of the plate and garnish with the remaining strawberry slices and the mint leaf. Eat straight away.

sally Cunningham invented this dish by accident when trying to get her cheesecake to set. Although this dessert looks and tastes decadent, it is relatively low in fat and sugar, so you can satisfy your sweet tooth without feeling guilty.

SALLY'S JELLIED RASPBERRY CHEESECAKE

SERVES 8–12

300ml (½ pint) boiling water

2 x 11.5g sachets sugar-free raspberry jelly powder

300ml (½ pint) cold water

75g (3oz) butter

200g (7oz) oat biscuits, such as Hobnobs, crushed

200g (7oz) extra light cream cheese

250g (8oz) mascarpone cheese

200g (7oz) raspberries, well drained if frozen, plus extra for decoration

Pour 150ml (¼ pint) boiling water into a heatproof bowl and stir in 1 sachet of the jelly powder. When the crystals have dissolved, top up with 150ml (¼ pint) cold water. Set aside to cool, but do not allow to set. (If it does start setting, warm briefly in the microwave.)

Melt the butter in a saucepan and stir in the crushed biscuits. Mix well, then press into the bottom of a 20cm (8in) springform cake tin. Place in the fridge.

Meanwhile, mix the cream cheese and mascarpone in a bowl, then add the cooled, still-liquid jelly and beat until smooth. Gently stir in half the raspberries (try not to crush them), and pour this mixture over the biscuit base. Place in the fridge to set – about 1 hour.

Make up the second sachet of jelly in the same way as the first, then add the remaining raspberries. Place on one side until just starting to set, then pour the jelly over the cheesecake. Chill in the fridge until set. Run a palette knife around the cheesecake, then unmould from the tin and slide gently on to a serving plate. Decorate around the edge of the cheesecake with the extra raspberries and enjoy with some single cream.

MALTON MESS

IN BRANDYSNAP BASKETS

SERVES 6

3–4 stalks rhubarb, chopped into 2.5cm (1in) lengths

2–3 tbsp soft brown sugar

3–4 tbsp raspberry liqueur, such as Raisthorpe Manor Raspberry Gin Liqueur

300ml (½ pint) double cream

300ml (½ pint) thick Greek yoghurt

225g (7½oz) raspberries, plus extra for decoration

For the meringues

2 large egg whites

pinch of cream of tartar

115g (3¾oz) caster sugar

1 tsp vinegar

Preheat the oven to 140°C/275°F/Gas Mark 1. Line a baking sheet with baking parchment for the meringues. For the brandysnaps, line a baking sheet with a silicon mat or baking parchment and oil lightly. Grease the outside of 6 large ramekins.

First make the meringues. Put the egg whites and cream of tartar in a large bowl and whisk until they are so stiff that they don't fall out when the bowl is turned upside down. Add the sugar about 25g (1oz) at a time, whisking well between each addition, then whisk in the vinegar.

Place heaped tablespoons of the mixture on the prepared sheet and bake for 1–1¼ hours, until crisp and firm. Allow to cool completely before gently lifting off the parchment. If not using them straight away, store in an airtight container until needed.

To make the brandysnap baskets, increase the oven temperature to 180°C/350°F/Gas Mark 4. Put the butter, sugar and syrup in a saucepan and melt over a low heat. Remove from the heat and stir in the flour, ginger and lemon zest. Set aside to cool.

Place heaped dessertspoons of the brandysnap mixture on the prepared sheet, spacing them well apart. Bake for 8–10 minutes, until they have spread into golden, lacy circles. Allow to cool for 1 minute then, working quickly, carefully lift off the circles and gently push each one over an upside-down ramekin, moulding

For the brandysnap baskets
sunflower oil for greasing

50g (2oz) butter

115g (3¾oz) caster sugar

50g (2oz) golden syrup

50g (2oz) plain flour

½ tsp ground ginger

½ tsp lemon zest

To serve
lemon balm sprigs

200g (7oz) good-quality white chocolate, shaved into curls (use a sharp knife held at a 45-degree angle)

it to shape. Allow to cool, then turn out and set aside. If not using them straight away, store in an airtight container until needed. (There may be more baskets than required for this recipe, so just keep them for another time.)

To make the mess, increase the oven temperature to 190°C/375°F/ Gas Mark 5. Place the rhubarb in a shallow baking dish, sprinkle in the sugar and liqueur, stir gently and bake for 20–30 minutes, until the rhubarb is soft, but still holding its shape. Pour the juice into a jug and chill the rhubarb for 1 hour. (The juice makes a refreshing summer drink if cooled and poured over ice cubes, then topped up with lemonade – and possibly a little more gin added.)

Whip the cream into soft peaks, then fold in the yoghurt, followed by the raspberries and rhubarb. Crumble in the meringues, leaving the pieces quite chunky, and mix well to combine.

Pile generous portions of the mess into the brandysnap baskets and decorate with the extra raspberries, the lemon balm and white chocolate curls. Serve as soon as possible to keep the meringue crunchy.

Global Harmony is a world music community choir based in Melton Mowbray. Choir member Mary Ward adapted this recipe from one she was given in Georgia, USA, over 30 years ago. Liz Underhill, the choir leader, says the group like to sing a Jamaican calypso-style song with their pie as it goes so well with the ingredients.

GLOBAL HARMONY'S NO-CRUST COCONUT PIE

SERVES 8

50g (2oz) margarine, plus extra for greasing

225g (7½oz) caster sugar

75g (3oz) self-raising flour, sifted

4 large eggs, beaten

115g (3¾oz) flaked or desiccated coconut

juice and zest of 1 lime

475ml (16fl oz) milk

Preheat the oven to 180°C/350°F/Gas Mark 4. Lightly grease a 25cm (10in) deep pie dish.

Put the margarine and sugar in a bowl and beat together until pale and fluffy. Mix in the flour, then add the eggs one at a time, beating constantly. Fold in the coconut, lime juice and zest, then stir in the milk. Pour the mixture into the prepared pie dish and bake for 50–60 minutes, or until the top is firm and golden brown.

Set aside to cool slightly before cutting into wedges and serving warm or cold.

When pushed for time before a birthday party father-of-three Mark Hart came up with this ingenious combination of two favourite recipes: classic trifle and baked egg custard tart. Everyone loved the cream-topped combination of strawberries, sponge and custard all baked in a pastry shell.

BAKED TRIFLE

SERVES 8-10

1.25kg (2½lb) strawberries, hulled

1 tbsp caster sugar (or to taste)

For the cakes
3 large eggs

2 tsp vanilla extract

175g (6oz) soft unsalted butter, plus extra for greasing

175g (6oz) caster sugar

175g (6oz) self-raising flour, sifted

pinch of salt

For the pastry
300g (10oz) plain flour, sifted, plus extra for dusting

150g (5oz) unsalted butter, cubed

40g (1½oz) caster sugar

2 eggs, beaten

3 tbsp milk

For the custard
8 egg yolks

75g (3oz) caster sugar

seeds from 2 vanilla pods

500ml (17fl oz) whipping cream

For the topping
300ml (½ pint) whipping cream

seeds from 1 vanilla pod

3 tbsp icing sugar, sifted

2 tsp grated dark chocolate

Preheat the oven to 180°C/350°F/Gas Mark 4. Butter two 20cm (8in) loose-bottomed cake tins.

First make the cakes, preferably the day before needed, as they need time to cool. Put the eggs and vanilla extract in a bowl and beat together. Put the butter and sugar in a separate bowl and beat together. Slowly beat in the egg mixture until light and fluffy. Fold in the flour and salt. Divide the mixture between the prepared tins and bake for about 20 minutes, or until a skewer inserted in the centre comes out clean. Set aside to cool in the tins, then turn out on to a wire rack until completely cold.

To make the pastry, put the flour and butter in a bowl and rub together or process until the mixture resembles breadcrumbs. Stir in the sugar, then add half the beaten egg, cutting it in with a knife. Gradually add the milk, a little at a time, until a dough forms. Roll into a ball, wrap in cling film and chill for 30 minutes.

On a lightly floured work surface, roll out the pastry and use to line a round 23cm (9in) pie dish, leaving about a 1.5 cm (¾in) overhang. Prick the base of the pastry case with a fork, then chill for 10 minutes or until firm to the touch.

Line the pastry case with a sheet of crumpled greaseproof paper and fill it with ceramic baking beans, dried pulses or rice, and bake (still at 180°C/350°F/Gas Mark 4) for 15 minutes. Remove the paper and beans, then brush with the remaining beaten egg and return to the oven for a further 5 minutes. Set aside to cool, and lower the oven temperature to 150°C/300°F/Gas Mark 2. Trim off any overhanging pastry.

To make the custard, combine the egg yolks, sugar, vanilla seeds and cream in a bowl. (There is no need to cook the mixture at this point because it will be baked.)

Lightly mash the strawberries in a bowl (don't pulp them), then strain through a sieve, reserving the juice – you will need about 4 tablespoons of it. Stir the sugar into the strawberries and set aside.

If the top of the cold cakes is not flat, use a bread knife to cut them level. Discard the tops, then cut the cakes horizontally through the middle so you have 4 circles each about 1cm (½in) thick.

Put a 1cm (½in) layer of strawberries in the bottom of the pastry case. Place a circle of sponge on top, and pour over just enough custard to cover the sponge. Repeat this process, finishing with the final sponge on top, until all the ingredients have been used. Bake in the oven for 35–40 minutes, until just set (the custard should still have a slight wobble). Pour the reserved strawberry juice over the top and set aside to cool in the tin. When cold, remove from the tin and place on a serving plate.

To make the topping, combine the cream, vanilla seeds and sugar in a bowl and whip to soft peaks. Using a palette knife, spread this mixture over the cake. Sprinkle the chocolate over the top and serve straight away.

Skiffle band Route 66 are based at Bilton Grange Community Centre in Hull. Joan (washboard), Jamie (tambourine), Daryl (tea chest bass), Ian (harmonica and vocals), Peter (drums), Pete (bass and double bass), Paul and John (guitar) are kept in check by Joan and Brenda. Working with the fruit they harvest from the community garden and support from their cookery volunteer, Annika Wardale, this recipe has been devised to 'hit the spot' after a band session.

FRUIT 66 SPECIAL BREAD & BUTTER PUDDING

SERVES 15

400g (13oz) brioche loaf

115g (3¾oz) butter

300ml (½ pint) double cream

300ml (½ pint) full-fat milk

4 tbsp caster sugar

1 vanilla pod, split open lengthways and seeds scraped out

1 tsp vanilla extract

6 large egg yolks

½ tsp freshly grated nutmeg

4 tbsp bourbon

150g (5oz) blueberries or other summer fruit

2 tbsp demerara sugar

Preheat the oven to 160°C/325°F/Gas Mark 3. Line a 15-hole muffin tin with paper cases.

Cut the brioche into slices 2.5cm (1in) thick and lightly butter each side. Cut each slice into six roughly equal cubes and set aside.

Place the cream, milk and caster sugar in a saucepan and warm over a low heat. Add the vanilla pod and seeds plus the extract and allow to infuse (it is ready when you can smell the vanilla). Take the pan off the heat, pour the mixture into a bowl and remove the vanilla pod. Whisk in the egg yolks, then the nutmeg and bourbon. Place the cubed brioche in the mixture and stir well, allowing it to soak up the liquid. Stir in the blueberries, taking care not to break them, and set aside for 10 minutes.

Spoon the brioche mixture into the paper cases and sprinkle each one with a little of the demerara sugar. Place the muffin tin in a roasting tin and pour a shallow depth of boiling water around it – this will help the puddings to remain moist and cook evenly. Bake for 20 minutes, until risen and brown. Transfer to a wire rack to cool.

Reverend Linda Boon's late Great Auntie Madge was famed for her carrot cake, and this recipe is still made by Linda and her daughters for family occasions and charity cake sales. The recipe is easy to scale up or down and tastes great with other dried fruit and spices such as chopped preserved ginger or a pinch of chilli flakes.

GREAT AUNTIE MADGE'S CARROT CAKE

SERVES 6–8

200g (7oz) soft brown sugar

200g (7oz) sunflower oil, plus extra for greasing (optional)

3 eggs, lightly beaten

200g (7oz) self-raising flour

1½ tsp baking powder

2 tsp ground cinnamon

½ tsp salt

200g (7oz) carrots, finely grated

200g (7oz) dried fruit and nuts (e.g. sultanas, raisins, walnut pieces, chopped pecans, etc.), plus extra walnuts to decorate

For the icing
125g (4oz) soft butter

225g (8oz) cream cheese

450g (14½oz) icing sugar

1 tsp vanilla extract

Preheat the oven to 150°C /300°F/Gas Mark 2. Line a 20cm (8in) round cake tin with baking parchment, or grease thoroughly and sprinkle with flour.

Put the sugar and oil in a bowl and beat together until pale and thick. Add the eggs and beat again until the texture is light and mousse-like.

In a separate bowl, combine the flour, baking powder, cinnamon and salt, then sift into the egg mixture and fold together lightly. Stir in the carrots and fruit and nut mixture, then pour into the prepared cake tin and level the top.

Bake for 1½–2 hours, until a skewer inserted in the centre of the cake comes out clean. Set aside until cool enough to handle, then turn out of the tin and place on a wire rack until completely cold.

Once the cake is cold, combine all the icing ingredients in a bowl and beat together until smooth. Spread the icing over the cake , decorate with walnuts and serve straight away.

This banana loaf cake captures the flavours of Grenada, where Sarah still went on holiday a few years ago with her aunt. Sarah loves making cakes for her family, especially her granddad, who has always encouraged her to be creative with her baking.

A TASTE OF SUNSHINE

SERVES 12

300g (10oz) plain flour

1 tsp bicarbonate of soda

125g (4oz) margarine, plus extra for greasing

250g (8oz) caster sugar

4-5 slightly overripe bananas

2 eggs

½ tsp vanilla extract

75ml (3fl oz) milk, mixed with 1½ tsp lemon juice

¼ tsp finely grated nutmeg

¾ tbsp finely grated 100% cacao

1 tsp ground mixed spice

pinch of ground cinnamon (optional)

Preheat the oven to 180°C/350°F/Gas Mark 4. Grease a 1kg (2lb) loaf tin and line with greaseproof paper.

Sift the flour and bicarbonate of soda into a bowl. In a separate bowl, beat the margarine and sugar until light and fluffy.

Mash the bananas in a bowl. Add the eggs, vanilla extract and milk mixture, stir well, then pour into the creamed margarine and whisk together. Fold in the flour mixture using a perforated metal spoon. Add the nutmeg, cacao, mixed spice and cinnamon (if using) and fold in lightly but thoroughly. Pour into the prepared tin.

Bake in the centre of the oven for about 20 minutes, until the loaf is risen and golden brown, then cover loosely with foil and bake for a further 20-30 minutes, or until a skewer inserted into the middle of the cake comes out clean.

Turn out of the tin immediately and remove the greaseproof paper. Leave to stand on a wire rack until cooled.

The inspiration for Marcelle Burden's cake comes from her French grandmother, who used all sorts of wild plants in her cooking, making delicious food from simple, natural ingredients that were freely available. Marcelle picks nettles from a meadow on her smallholding.

NETTLE CAKE

SERVES 8–10

butter for greasing

20g (¾oz) nettle tips, coarsely chopped

1 scant tsp ground mixed spice

1 scant tsp ground cinnamon

1 tsp grated fresh ginger

75g (3oz) sultanas

175g (6oz) natural yoghurt or crème fraîche

135g (4½oz) raw light brown cane sugar

150ml (¼ pint) light olive oil or sunflower oil

150ml (¼ pint) runny honey

200g (7oz) self-raising flour, plus extra for dusting

115g (3¾oz) wholemeal self-raising flour

2 large eggs, beaten

50g (2oz) bramble jelly

1 tsp granulated sugar for dusting

Preheat oven to 190°C/375°F/Gas Mark 5. Butter and flour two 20cm (8in) round cake tins.

Put the nettles, spices, sultanas, yoghurt, sugar, oil and honey in a bowl and mix well. Stir in the flours, then add the eggs and mix again. Divide the mixture equally between the prepared tins. Bake on the top shelf of the oven for 20 minutes, then lower the heat to 160°C/325°F/Gas Mark 3 and bake for a further 10–20 minutes, until a skewer inserted in the centre comes out clean. Allow to cool in the tins for 10 minutes, then turn on to a wire rack to cool completely.

To serve, sandwich the cakes together with the bramble jelly and dust the top with sugar.

NORTH-WEST

NORTH-WEST

The first day of the Harrogate Autumn Flower Show in Yorkshire was the scene of our North-West heat. Every year visitors to the Show look forward to the fiercely contested competition between vegetable growers for the biggest vegetables. There was a great atmosphere with plenty for all the contestants and their families to do while they waited for their turn to be judged. That's if the judges could be found, as they kept sneaking off to admire the supersized veg!

As you'd expect from this region, it was the battle of the hotpots. Traditionally, this Lancashire lamb stew, topped with sliced potatoes, was put into the oven and left to cook slowly all day. There are many different variations on the classic recipe, some with mushrooms or even oysters. This heat featured both classic and contemporary recipes, including the one in this book: Corned Beef & Bacon Hotpot.

The contestants came up trumps with some amazing international dishes too, among them Lamb Kefta with Giant Cous Cous and the Middle Eastern soup, Kubbah Hamute.

Happily for the many pie-lovers among us, this was the day for a plethora of pies: Granddad's; Game; Cottage and Banoffee. Representing some of Scotland's famous regional ingredients were the intriguingly named Wonderfully Wicked Whisky Sausages and Sausage & Haggis Casserole. And who could forget that amazing character, the town crier and his recipe for Cream Horns? What dish could be more appropriate for a town crier than that?

Take a really unpopular vegetable and make something utterly delicious with it — that's what greengrocer Chris Eden did 12 years ago and it's still in high demand from friends and family. The Thai flavours and chestnuts work brilliantly with the Brussels sprouts, and it's a wonderfully warming soup for wintry days.

BRUSSELS SPROUT, CHESTNUT & COCONUT SOUP

SERVES 6

1 tbsp olive oil

1 tsp cumin seeds

6 shallots, finely chopped

3 garlic cloves, finely chopped

175ml (6fl oz) white wine

175g (6oz) cooked peeled chestnuts

2 floury potatoes, roughly diced

½ tsp freshly grated nutmeg

½ tsp cayenne pepper

1 tsp ground turmeric

900ml (1½ pints) hot vegetable stock

500g (1lb) Brussels sprouts, halved

115g (3¾oz) creamed coconut

salt and freshly ground black pepper

Put the oil in a large, heavy-based saucepan over a medium heat and briefly fry the cumin seeds. Add the shallots and fry for 3–4 minutes, until softened but not coloured. Add the garlic and wine, bring to the boil, then add the chestnuts, potatoes, nutmeg, cayenne pepper, turmeric and stock and simmer for 10 minutes.

Add the sprouts and cook for 8–10 minutes, or until both the potatoes and sprouts are tender. Stir in the creamed coconut.

Pour the soup into a blender and whiz until smooth, adding more stock if it is too thick. Season well and serve with a swirl of crème fraîche and a sprinkling of toasted flaked almonds.

This budget-friendly dish has been passed down to David Barski from his mother, and he cooks it for his own family at least twice a month. The longer you cook it the better it tastes – and David likes to serve it with some crunchy pickled red cabbage.

CORNED BEEF & BACON HOTPOT

SERVES 6

1 tsp butter for greasing

2 beef stock cubes

salt and white pepper

300ml (½ pint) boiling water

750g (1½lb) potatoes, cut into 5mm (¼in) slices

625g (1¼lb) carrots, cut into 2.5mm (⅛in) slices

340g can of chilled corned beef, cut into 2.5mm (⅛in) slices

3–4 onions sliced

8 rashers of bacon, each cut into 3 pieces

400g can of chopped tomatoes

Preheat the oven to 220°C/425°F/Gas Mark 7. Butter a 2.75 litre (5 pint) casserole dish.

Crumble the stock cubes into a jug, add a pinch of salt and pepper, then pour in the boiling water. Stir well until the cubes have dissolved.

Place a double layer of potato slices inside the casserole dish. Follow this with a double layer of carrot slices, then a layer using half the corned beef slices. Cover with a layer of onions, followed by half the bacon, then half the tomatoes. Season with a little salt and pepper, then repeat the layers until all the ingredients are used up (or the dish is full). The final layer should be potatoes topped with a little bit of tomato. Pour the stock over the top, then press down the layers with your hands, and add enough water to half-fill the dish.

Cover and place in the oven for 1 hour. Press the layers down with the back of a spoon so that the juices submerge the top, then cover and return to the oven for another 30 minutes, or until all the vegetables are cooked. You can test for this by inserting a sharp knife into the casserole – if it goes in dead easily, it's done.

Serve with pickled beetroot or red cabbage and chunks of crusty white bread.

> *Alan Herron uses locally sourced game for this flavoursome pie, and the damsons for his damson jelly come from a friend's garden. Any combination of game works well, but take care with grouse as too much can overwhelm the other flavours. Alan proposed to his girlfriend with a Hula Hoop at the North-west heat — and she said 'yes'!*

GAME PIE & DAMSON JELLY

SERVES 4–6 AND MAKES TWO 500G (1LB) JARS OF DAMSON JELLY

500g (1lb) assorted game meat, e.g. breasts from 2 grouse, 2 partridge, 2 pigeon and 2 pheasant, each cut into 3.5cm (1½in) dice, carcasses and legs reserved

1 tbsp plain flour seasoned with a pinch of salt and pepper

1 tbsp olive oil

125g (4oz) rare breed pork shoulder, coarsely minced (ask your butcher to do this)

125g (4oz) streaky bacon, finely chopped

¼ tsp freshly ground white pepper

½ tsp freshly ground black pepper

¼ tsp ground mace

leaves from 2 sprigs of thyme, chopped

¾ tsp salt

First make the damson jelly. Preheat the oven to its lowest setting and warm the sugar in a dish for about 15 minutes. Put the fruit and the water clinging to it in a heavy-based saucepan and place over a moderate heat until the damsons start breaking down. Slowly bring to the boil, stirring and pressing the fruit to release the juice. After about 10 minutes, it should have released as much juice as it is going to. Add the warmed sugar and stir until dissolved, then boil rapidly for 8 minutes.

Line a large nylon sieve with a double layer of muslin and suspend it over a bowl. Tip in the fruit mixture and let the juice drip through of its own accord (pressing will lead to a clouded jelly). Pour the liquid into warmed, sterilised jars (see Tip, page 57), then cover with waxed discs and seal tightly. Remember to label and date the jars. The jelly can be used immediately, but the flavours will develop with age.

To make the jelly stock, tightly pack all the ingredients for it in a large saucepan and cover with cold water. Bring to the boil, removing any scum as it rises to the surface, then simmer over a very low heat for at least 3½ hours (4½ is better). Strain into a jug – you should have about 900ml (1½ pints) – then cool and refrigerate in a covered container. The liquid will set into a jelly.

For the damson jelly
1kg (2lb) sugar

1kg (2lb) damsons

For the jelly stock
1 pig's trotter, split (ask your butcher to do this)

reserved carcasses and legs from the game meat

½ onion, finely chopped

4 juniper berries, lightly crushed

1 bay leaf

6 sprigs of thyme

4 peppercorns

For the pastry
50g (2oz) lard, diced

50g (2oz) butter, diced, plus extra for greasing

125ml (4fl oz) water

225g (7½oz) plain flour, plus extra for dusting

¾ tsp salt

2 eggs, beaten in 2 separate bowls

To make the pastry, put the lard, butter and 100ml (3½fl oz) of the water into a saucepan and heat gently until the fats have melted. Do not allow to boil. Place the flour and salt in a bowl, make a well in the centre and add one of the eggs. Stir gently with a spatula until half mixed, then pour in the melted fat and mix to form a soft dough. Add the remaining water if the dough seems too dry. Knead gently for just long enough to bring the mixture together, then roll into a ball, wrap in cling film and chill for 1 hour.

Preheat the oven to 180°C/350°F/Gas Mark 4. Butter a shallow 20cm (8in) loose-bottomed pie tin, preferably non-stick.

Take two-thirds of the chilled dough, place on a lightly floured work surface and roll into a circle large enough to line the prepared tin. Trim the excess pastry, leaving about 1cm (½in) overhanging the rim. Roll the reserved pastry into a circle large enough to cover the dish. Set both aside.

Dust the game meat with the seasoned flour. Heat the oil in a frying pan and quickly sear the meat in batches until the edges are brown. Transfer to a bowl and add the pork shoulder, bacon, white and black pepper, mace, thyme, salt and 2 tablespoons of the jellied stock. Mix well.

Pack the meat mixture into the pastry case up to the rim of the tin, making it slightly higher in the centre. Brush a little of the remaining beaten egg on the overhanging pastry and around the edge of the pastry lid. Put the lid on the pie and crimp the eggy edges together to seal. Cut a hole about the size of a 1p coin in the centre of the lid and brush the top with beaten egg.

Put the pie on a baking sheet and bake for 20 minutes. Lower the heat to 150°C/300°F/Gas Mark 2 and bake for another hour. Push the pie out of the tin, keeping the metal base in place, and brush beaten egg all around the sides. Return to the oven for 15 minutes to brown the sides, covering them with foil if they brown too quickly. Transfer the pie, still on the metal base, to a wire rack and leave to cool for 1 hour.

Gently warm the jellied stock so that it becomes liquid and pour this into the warm pie through the steam hole. I use a large syringe to do this, but you could use a small funnel and a jug if you've got a steady hand. When the pie is filled right to the top, set aside until cold, then refrigerate. (When I have the time, I top up the pie with liquid jellied stock every few hours to ensure it fills all the cavities above and within the meat filling.)

To serve, allow the pie to reach room temperature before scoffing it with a dollop of damson jelly.

Kirsty Couper has been passionate about food since she was young and loves to cook with fresh, seasonal produce. This zingy dish has become a firm favourite amongst her family and friends due to its vibrant flavours and colours.

MINT, PEA & LIME RISOTTO
WITH LEMONY CHARGRILLED ASPARAGUS

SERVES 8

125g (4oz) butter

6 tbsp olive oil

2 large onions, finely chopped

6 celery stalks, finely chopped

½ large head of garlic, cloves separated and finely grated

400g (13oz) arborio rice

250ml (8fl oz) dry white wine

1.8 litres (3 pints) chicken stock

625g (1¼lb) frozen peas

leaves from 3 large bunches of mint

zest of 8 lemons, juice of 3

juice of 2 limes

salt and freshly ground black pepper

250g (8oz) Parmesan cheese, finely grated

mint flowers, to garnish (optional)

For the asparagus
20 asparagus spears, woody parts discarded

1 tbsp olive oil

zest of 1 lemon

Heat the butter and 4 tablespoons of the oil in a large frying pan. Add the onions and celery and fry over a gentle heat for a few minutes. Add the garlic and cook for a further 12–15 minutes, stirring occasionally, until the onion and celery soften but do not colour.

Stir in the rice, coating it in the butter. Increase the heat to medium-high, then add the wine and stir until it evaporates.

Add the stock, a ladleful at a time, stirring constantly until the rice has absorbed the liquid. Continue cooking for about 20 minutes, until the rice is al dente and creamy, not dry.

In the meantime, cook the peas in boiling water for 2 minutes, then drain and place in a blender or food processor. Add the mint, reserving a few small leaves for decoration, then add the remaining oil, half of the lemon zest, plus the lime juice and all but 1 tablespoon of the lemon juice. Whiz until the mint has been incorporated and the mixture is a slightly chunky texture.

Season the risotto to taste, then add the remaining lemon zest and all but a handful of the Parmesan. Fold in the pea and mint mixture.

For the asparagus, heat a griddle pan until very hot. Brush the asparagus with the oil and sprinkle with the lemon zest. Place in the hot pan until charred on all sides, then transfer to a bowl and add the reserved tablespoon of lemon juice. Transfer the asparagus to a chopping board and cut on the diagonal into 5cm (2in) pieces. Set the tips aside and fold the stalks into the risotto.

Garnish the finished risotto with the reserved mint leaves, asparagus tips, mint flowers (if using) and remaining Parmesan and serve straight away.

Hannah Bowie-McLean's grandparents left Iraq in the 1950s, bringing this traditional recipe with them. This version has Hannah's personal slant, but stays true to its Assyrian-comfort-food roots of a spicy minced beef stuffing encased in rice flour and minced beef dough, cooked in a fragrant paprika-spiced soup.

KUBBAH HAMUTE

SERVES 4

1 tsp olive oil

1 onion, finely chopped

400g can of chopped tomatoes

2 tsp ground paprika

leaves from 1 handful of mint

2 chicken stock cubes

1 heaped tbsp tomato purée

1 swede, cubed

juice of 1 lemon

1 tsp ground coriander

1.8 litres (3 pints) boiling water

First make the dough. Put the beef, ground rice and a little salt and pepper into a blender or food processor, then gradually dribble in the water while pulsing, until you get a smooth, soft, bread-like dough; it should not be sticky or dry and cracked. If it is too wet, it will disintegrate when cooked. Leave to stand for at least 30 minutes while you prepare the stuffing.

Heat the oil in a pan and soften the onion and garlic in it for about 5 minutes. Transfer to a plate. Now fry the beef until brown, then return the onion and garlic to the pan and throw in the spices. Stir and fry for a further 5 minutes, until the meat is cooked through. Add the parsley, then set aside to cool.

To make the soup, heat the oil in a large saucepan and soften the onion. Add all the other ingredients and bring to the boil.

For the dough

250g (8oz) lean minced beef

250g (8oz) ground rice

salt and freshly ground black pepper

150–300ml (¼–½ pint) water

flour, for dusting

For the stuffing

1 tsp olive oil

1 large onion, finely chopped

2 garlic cloves, minced

250g (8oz) finely minced beef

2 tsp hot curry powder

2 tsp garam masala

large handful of parsley, chopped

Meanwhile, knead the dough on a lightly floured surface for 1 minute, then take small pieces and roll into balls slightly smaller than a golf ball. Press your thumb into each ball, then spoon some of the stuffing into each dent, packing in as much as you can while still being able to pinch the dough back together without the sides cracking. If cracks do appear, smooth them away with some water. Roll the balls back into shape, then flatten slightly into 'flying saucers'. These are your kubbah. (Any leftover stuffing can be added to the soup for extra flavour.)

When the soup starts to boil, add 4–5 kubbah at a time and wait a couple of minutes, until they float to the surface, before you add any more. Do not add too many at once as this will reduce the temperature of the soup and make the kubbah disintegrate. The soup is done when all the kubbah have risen to the surface and the swede is soft when pierced with a sharp knife – about 20 minutes. The soup will thicken during cooking.

An active member of Walmsley Church Amateur Operatic & Dramatic Society, William 'Donny' Howcroft took to cooking after being in hospital for many months almost 20 years ago. He and his wife Nora did all the catering for his 80th birthday party, and he created this recipe especially for the occasion.

SMOKED SALMON CHEESECAKE

SERVES 8-10

500ml (17fl oz) milk

165g (5½oz) salmon, skinless

9g sachet of gelatine

125ml (4fl oz) water

200g (7oz) smoked salmon

zest of 1 lemon

115g (3¾oz) mascarpone, at room temperature

400g (13oz) cream cheese, at room temperature

For the base

75g (3oz) butter

165g (5½oz) oatcake biscuits, crushed to fine crumbs

½ tsp dried dill

For the lemon jelly

9g sachet of gelatine

125ml (4fl oz) water

85ml (3¼fl oz) lemon juice

2 tbsp caster sugar

For the topping

8 lemon slices, peel and pith removed

8 tiger prawns

50g (2oz) smoked salmon

sprigs of dill, to decorate (optional)

First make the base. Melt the butter in a saucepan, then take off the heat and mix in the biscuit crumbs and dill. Place a 20cm (8in) flan ring on a flat serving plate and tip in the crumb mixture. Using a flat-bottomed tumbler, press the crumbs down evenly inside the ring, then place in the fridge while you make the topping.

To make the filling, bring the milk to the boil in a saucepan. Add the fresh salmon and simmer for 10 minutes. Discard the milk and set the fish aside to cool.

Put the gelatine in a jug with the water and microwave until dissolved, taking care not to let it boil. Alternatively, sprinkle the gelatine over the same amount of hot water and stir briskly until dissolved. Place the jug in a bowl of iced water to cool, but do not allow the gelatine to set.

Put the smoked salmon, fresh salmon and lemon zest in a blender or food processor and whiz until combined to a rough texture. Pour the mixture into a large bowl, add the mascarpone, cream cheese and cooled gelatine and whisk together. Spoon the mixture on to the chilled biscuit base, smooth the surface, then place in the fridge and chill for 20 minutes.

To make the lemon jelly, prepare the gelatine as before. When cool but not set, add the lemon juice and another 85ml (3¼fl oz) cold water.

Arrange the lemon slices evenly over the chilled cheesecake, then pour the cool lemon jelly over the surface. Return to the fridge for 4 hours or overnight, until set.

Decorate the cheesecake with the tiger prawns, smoked salmon and sprigs of dill, If liked, before serving.

This unusual recipe was born out of necessity when Jack Stride found himself buying ingredients on a budget to cook dinner for his housemates. Combining what looked good from the discount aisle of the supermarket with some leftover whisky, he set about creating a dish that went down an absolute storm!

ROAST BELLY OF PORK
WITH SWEET POTATO HASH & CHILLI JAM 'JUS'

SERVES 2

500g (1lb) belly of pork, cut into 4 strips

salt and freshly ground black pepper

2 sweet potatoes, chopped

1 tbsp butter

½ tsp cumin

75g (3oz) corned beef, crumbled

¼ red chilli

115g (3¾oz) strawberry jam

60ml (2½fl oz) blended malt whisky

1 sweet pepper, deseeded and finely diced

sugar (optional)

Preheat the oven to 190°C/375°F/Gas Mark 5.

Score the fat on the pork, rub with salt and season with pepper. Place on a lipped baking sheet or in a roasting tin and roast for 45-60 minutes.

Place the sweet potatoes in a large pan of water, bring to the boil and cook for 15 minutes, or until tender. Drain well, then mash with the butter and cumin. Stir in the corned beef.

Place the chilli, jam and whisky in a bowl and whiz together using a stick blender. Add the pepper and sugar to taste (if using). Transfer to a saucepan, bring to the boil and cook for 1-2 minutes.

To serve, place a large spoonful of the sweet potato hash on 2 serving plates, arrange the belly pork on or beside it and spoon over the chilli jam 'jus'.

GRANDAD'S MEAT & POTATO PIE

SERVES 6-8

600g (1lb 2oz) lean steak, trimmed and cubed

3-4 onions, diced

1.2 litres (2 pints) beef stock

salt and freshly ground black pepper

10-12 large potatoes (about 2kg /4lb), diced into small cubes

For the pastry
250g (8oz) plain flour, plus extra for dusting

1 tsp salt

125g (4oz) butter, cubed

125g (4oz) lard, cubed

1 egg whisked with 3 tbsp milk, to glaze

Preheat the oven to 220°C/425°F/Gas Mark 7.

Put the steak and onions into a large ovenproof casserole dish, add enough of the stock to cover, and season with salt and pepper. Place in the oven, and when the liquid begins to boil, lower the heat to 180°C/350°F/Gas Mark 4, cover and cook for 2½-3 hours, or until the meat is tender. (It can also be cooked at a lower temperature for a longer time if you have things to do.)

To make the pastry, sift the flour and salt into a bowl, add the butter and lard, then rub together with your fingertips until the mixture resembles breadcrumbs. Add water a little at a time, mixing it in with a knife, until a dough forms. Roll into a ball, wrap in cling film and chill for at least 20 minutes.

When the meat is tender, place the potatoes over it and top up with stock to cover. Return to the oven and increase the heat to 220°C/425°F/Gas Mark 7 until the liquid bubbles. At that point, lower the heat to 180°C/350°F/Gas Mark 4 and cook slowly for 1-1½ hours, until the potatoes are soft.

When ready, remove from the oven, mash the potatoes just a little with a fork and set aside to cool for 20 minutes.

On a lightly floured work surface, roll out the pastry large enough to cover the casserole dish. Brush the edges of the dish with some of the egg and milk mixture, place the pastry on top, then trim off the excess and cut into shapes to decorate the pie. Brush the surface with the egg and milk mixture and return to the oven for 20-30 minutes, or until the pastry has browned.

Serve with mushy peas, mashed carrots, red cabbage and pickles, and crusty bread and butter.

This dish was made by Gillian Lutas' dad, Norman Kay, who was a baker by trade and did most of the family cooking. Gillian loves cooking, and has made this recipe hundreds of times for all sorts of occasions. She sticks firmly to her late father's recipe, and every time she makes it she thinks of him.

It's the mash on top that makes Lisa Hutchings' cottage pie special – parsnips, swede and sweet potato joining the usual white potatoes to create a new take on this classic dish. Lisa makes her pie about once a fortnight and everyone she's made it for always asks for more!

COTTAGE PIE
WITH MIXED ROOT MASH

SERVES 6

2 tbsp vegetable oil

2 medium onions, sliced

200g (7oz) button mushrooms, sliced

500g (1lb) lean minced beef

4 beef stock cubes (reduce to 2 cubes for a less salty taste)

1 heaped tsp English mustard

1 heaped tsp garlic powder

1 heaped tbsp tomato purée

1 tsp dried mixed herbs

½ tsp freshly ground black pepper

225ml (7½fl oz) boiling water

salt

125g (4oz) frozen petit pois

For the topping
2 medium parsnips (about 225g/7½oz), chopped

200g (7oz) swede, finely chopped

3 medium King Edward potatoes (about 600g/1lb 2oz), chopped

2 medium sweet potatoes (about 275g/9oz), chopped

115g (3¾oz) butter

½ tsp white pepper

Preheat the oven to 180°C/350°F/Gas Mark 4.

Heat the oil in a large, deep frying pan over a medium heat, then brown the onions and mushrooms in it for about 10 minutes. Transfer to a plate and set aside.

Using the same pan, dry-fry the beef until brown, then add the fried onion mixture.

Crumble the stock cubes into a jug with the mustard, garlic powder, tomato purée, mixed herbs and pepper. Add the water and mix well. Taste and add more salt if necessary. Pour the stock into the beef mixture, bring to the boil, then simmer for 2–3 minutes. Remove from the heat and mix in the peas. Transfer to an ovenproof dish measuring about 27 x 23 x 9cm (11 x 9 x 4in) and set aside.

To make the topping, place the parsnips and swede in a large pan of boiling salted water and cook for 5 minutes. Add the rest of the root vegetables and cook for another 15–20 minutes, until soft. Drain, add the butter, pepper and salt and mash well. Gently spread the mash over the beef mixture and tease the top into a nice pattern using a fork. The more ridges you create, the more crispy bits there will be.

Place in the oven for about 40 minutes, or until golden brown and bubbling. Serve with steamed broccoli and carrot batons.

Baking fan Sanam Alam makes her banoffee pie without condensed milk — she creates her own caramel instead from cream, sugar and water. She likes to make her pie for special occasions, and it's become a family classic that everyone loves to eat.

SANAM'S BANOFFEE PIE

SERVES 12

175g (6oz) sugar

85ml (3¼fl oz) water

1 litre (1¾ pints) double cream

400g (13oz) digestive biscuits, finely crushed

200g (7oz) margarine, melted

4 medium bananas, sliced

2 tbsp icing sugar

1 tsp vanilla extract

40g (1½oz) chocolate, grated

Heat the sugar and water in a saucepan, tilting it to swirl them together (do not stir). Once they have turned deep brown, add half the cream and stir until smooth. Transfer to a bowl and set aside to cool for 2 hours.

Meanwhile, combine the biscuits and margarine in a bowl until the mixture has the consistency of wet sand. Tip into a 27cm (10½in) loose-bottomed tart tin and press down firmly over the base with the back of a spoon. Chill for at least 1 hour.

Pour the caramel mixture over the chilled biscuit base, then arrange the banana slices on top. Chill for another hour, or until the caramel has set.

Whip the remaining cream with the icing sugar and vanilla extract into medium peaks. Spread this over the pie, then sprinkle with the grated chocolate.

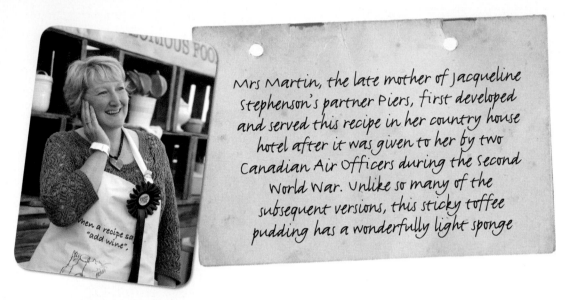

Mrs Martin, the late mother of Jacqueline Stephenson's partner Piers, first developed and served this recipe in her country house hotel after it was given to her by two Canadian Air Officers during the Second World War. Unlike so many of the subsequent versions, this sticky toffee pudding has a wonderfully light sponge

MRS MARTIN'S ORIGINAL STICKY TOFFEE PUDDING

SERVES 6

225g (7½oz) plain flour, plus extra for dusting

175g (6oz) stoned dates

300ml (½ pint) boiling water

1 tsp bicarbonate of soda

1 tsp vanilla extract

1 tsp baking powder

175g (6oz) granulated sugar

90g (3½oz) softened butter, plus extra for greasing

1 large egg, lightly beaten

65g (2½oz) brown sugar

2 tbsp double cream

Preheat the oven to 180°C/350°F/Gas Mark 4. Butter a 28 x 18cm (11 x 7in) cake tin.

Flour the dates lightly and chop them finely. Place in a heatproof bowl, pour the boiling water over them, then mix in the bicarbonate of soda and vanilla extract. Set aside to cool.

Sift the flour and baking powder into a bowl. Put the granulated sugar and 50g (2oz) of the butter in another bowl and cream together. Beat in the egg with a little of the flour for a couple of minutes, then add the rest of the flour. Stir in the date mixture and mix well.

Pour the mixture into the prepared tin and bake for about 40 minutes, until firm on top and a skewer inserted in the centre comes out clean.

To make the toffee, put the brown sugar, cream and remaining butter in a saucepan and heat together until the sugar has dissolved. Bring to the boil, then simmer for 3 minutes. Pour the toffee over the hot pudding and place under a hot grill until it bubbles. Watch it closely, as it can easily burn.

Serve with double cream or vanilla ice cream or both.

LEMON CRUNCH CAKE

SERVES 8-10

200g (7oz) gingernut biscuits, finely crushed

115g (3¾oz) spreadable butter, melted

25g (1oz) caster sugar

300ml (½ pint) double cream

397g can of condensed milk

zest of 3 lemons

175ml (6fl oz) lemon juice

seasonal berries for decoration

Combine the biscuits with the butter and sugar, then press the mixture firmly into the bottom of a 23cm (9in) springform cake tin. Place in the fridge for at least 1 hour.

Lightly whip the cream in a bowl until just holding its shape, then fold in the condensed milk, lemon zest and juice. Spoon the mixture over the biscuit base and chill for another hour.

To serve, unmould from the tin and decorate with a few handfuls of seasonal berries.

Post Card

CORRESPONDENCE   ADDRESS ONLY

Jennie Young's favourite recipe is this cake, which has been handed down the generations of her family. She remembers making it with her mum, and now makes it with her own kids from the handwritten recipe tucked into the back of her nan's old cookery book.

Cath Webb first baked this cake for her friend who had been diagnosed with breast cancer. It brought such a smile to her friend's face that she decided to bake a cake every day for a year and give it to someone to lift their spirits. Sometimes baking late into the night and even on a family camping trip, Cath's year of giving cakes has touched over 1,500 lives, no doubt bringing about plenty of smiles.

SMILE CAKE

SERVES 8

200g (7oz) soft butter, plus extra for greasing

200g (7oz) golden caster sugar

3 tbsp good-quality vanilla extract

3 large eggs (200g/7oz in total)

200g (7oz) self-raising flour

3 tbsp semi-skimmed milk

225g (7½oz) easy-to-spread strawberry jam

Taylor & Colledge vanilla bean dusting sugar, for dusting (if you can't buy this you can make your own by placing a vanilla pod in a jar of icing sugar and leaving to infuse for a week)

icing sugar, for dusting

Preheat the oven to 160°C/350°F/Gas Mark 3. Butter and flour two 19cm (7½in) sponge tins. Cut out 2 circles of card, each about the size of a £1 coin, for the eyes; and cut a crescent about 15cm (6in) long for the smiley mouth.

Put the butter and sugar in a bowl and beat until pale and fluffy. Add the vanilla extract (using a little more if you want a stronger vanilla flavour) and beat again.

Crack the eggs separately into a bowl. Beat them into the butter and sugar, then fold in the flour. Add the milk gradually, beating between each addition, until the mixture has a dropping consistency.

Divide the cake batter equally between the prepared tins and place in the oven for 24 minutes, or until golden, risen and firm to the touch. Turn the cakes on to a wire rack to cool.

Spread the jam on one of the cakes and place the other cake on top. Arrange the card cut-outs on the surface, then dust all over with the vanilla bean dusting sugar, followed by a fine dusting of icing sugar. Remove the templates using tweezers and give the cake to someone to make them smile.

CARROT CAKE

SERVES 8–10

250ml (8fl oz) groundnut oil or corn oil, plus extra for greasing

275g (9oz) brown sugar

3 medium carrots (about 250g/8oz in total), grated

3 eggs

125g (4oz) walnuts, chopped, plus extra halves for decoration

115g (3¾oz) raisins, chopped

375g (12oz) self-raising flour, sifted

½ tsp bicarbonate of soda

2 tsp ground mixed spice

1 tsp ground cinnamon

sugar carrot decorations

For the icing

75g (3oz) cream cheese

75g (3oz) soft unsalted butter

juice and zest of 1 lemon

350g (11½oz) icing sugar

Preheat the oven to 200°C/400°F/Gas Mark 6. Oil a 20cm (8in) deep, loose-bottomed cake tin and line it with greaseproof paper.

Put the oil and sugar in a small bowl and mix well. Add the carrots and eggs and mix again.

Place the remaining ingredients in a separate bowl and add the carrot mixture, stirring until well incorporated.

Transfer the mixture to the prepared tin and bake for 45–60 minutes, checking it after 35 minutes and covering it with a piece of parchment or foil if the top is getting too brown. The cake is ready when golden brown and a knife or skewer inserted in the middle comes out clean. Set aside to cool for 15–20 minutes, then turn on to a wire rack and leave until completely cold.

To make the icing, put all the ingredients for it in a bowl and beat until the mixture has a thick dropping consistency. Spread over the top and sides of the cake and decorate with the reserved walnut halves and the sugar carrots.

To serve, place the cake on a serving plate and enjoy with a cuppa and some gossip.

During the Second World War Mrs McNab was evacuated from Glasgow to stay with Muriel Readhead's grandparents in Lanarkshire. She gave this recipe to Muriel's grandmother, who taught Muriel how to bake. The handwritten recipe has been passed down to Muriel, who still loves baking and makes cakes regularly for church events.

MRS MCNAB'S
FRUIT LOAF

MAKES 1 LOAF

225g (7½oz) self-raising flour, sifted

1 tsp bicarbonate of soda

1 tsp ground ginger

1 tsp ground mixed spice

1 tsp ground cinnamon

115g (3¾oz) sultanas

90g (3½oz) margarine, plus extra for greasing

90g (3½oz) granulated sugar

1 tbsp golden syrup

1 tbsp black treacle

150ml (¼ pint) boiling water

Preheat the oven to 180°C/350°C/Gas Mark 4. Lightly grease a 1kg (2lb) loaf tin and line it with greaseproof paper.

Place the flour, bicarbonate of soda, spices and sultanas in a large bowl. In a separate bowl, cream together the margarine and sugar. Stir in the syrup and treacle, then add to the dry ingredients with the boiling water. Mix until thoroughly combined.

Transfer the cake batter to the prepared tin and bake for 1 hour, until a skewer inserted in the centre comes out clean. Loosely cover with foil, if needed, if the cake seems to be browning too quickly after 30–40 minutes. Turn on to a wire rack to cool, then cut into thick slices and serve.

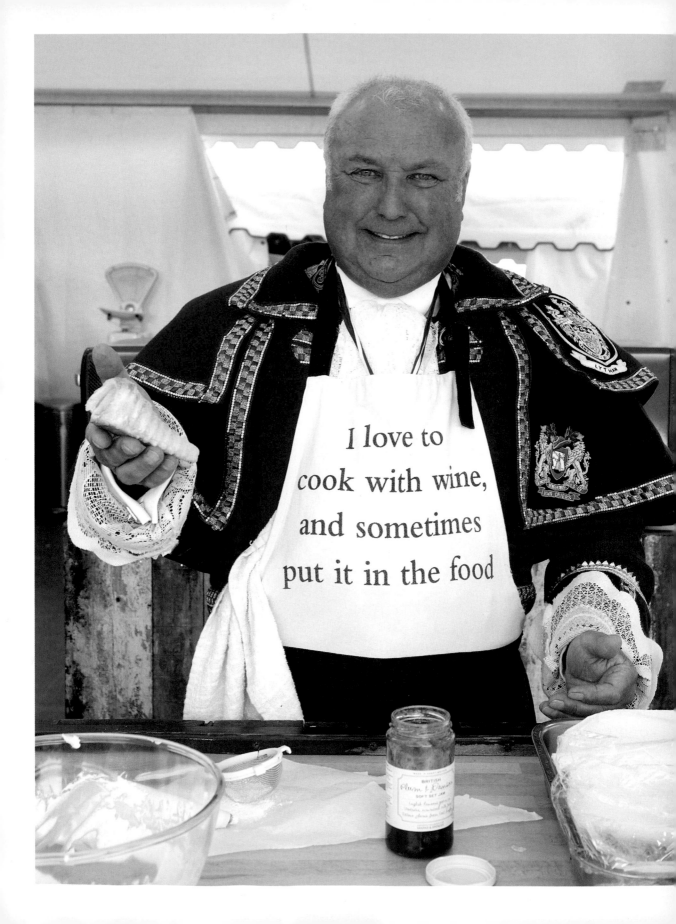

COLIN'S CREAM HORNS

MAKES 12

500g (1lb) plain flour, plus extra for dusting

375g (12oz) cold butter, cut into small cubes, plus extra for greasing

pinch of salt

250ml (8fl oz) cold water

1 egg, beaten

50g (2oz) caster sugar

4 tbsp jam or chocolate spread or other preferred filling

300ml (½ pint) double cream

25g (1oz) icing sugar

Sift the flour into a large bowl and add the butter and salt. Add the water and mix the ingredients gently until the dough becomes a rough lump. Wrap in cling film and chill for at least 30 minutes.

Place the dough on a lightly floured work surface and shape it into a brick-like slab, then roll it into a rectangle about 38 x 18cm (15 x 7in). With the narrow end nearest you, fold the bottom third up to the middle, then fold the top third over it. Roll out again to the same size as before, then turn through 90 degrees and repeat the folding and rolling process. Do this another 3 times (so 5 times in total), then wrap the pastry in cling film and chill for at least 4 hours but preferably overnight.

Preheat the oven to 200°C/400°F/Gas Mark 6. Lightly grease a baking sheet and the outside of 12 cream horn moulds.

Remove the pastry from the fridge and allow it to come to room temperature. Place it on a floured work surface and roll into a rectangle 50 x 30cm (20 x 13in) and about 5mm (¼in) thick. Cut 12 lengthways strips about 2.5cm (1in) wide.

Wind a strip of pastry around each cream horn mould, beginning at the tapered end and overlapping the pastry slightly as you work upwards. Do not to wrap it over the edge of the mould, or the pastry horn will be impossible to remove after baking without breaking it.

Brush the horns all over with the beaten egg and dip one side of each into caster sugar. Transfer them to the baking sheet with the sugared side facing upwards. Sprinkle a few drops of water on to the sheet and bake for 12–14 minutes, or until golden brown. Set aside to cool before gently twisting the horns off the moulds.

Drop 1 teaspoonful of jam or chocolate spread into each horn and gently smear it around the inside. Whip the double cream into stiff peaks, then spoon into a piping bag and pipe it into the horns, making a swirl effect at the top of each one.

To serve, dust with a little icing sugar and arrange on a beautiful china plate or cake stand.

Toastmaster and town crier Colin W. Ballard makes this recipe using the cream horn tins that belonged to his father William, who was a baker. When his father passed away, Colin's cousin Ingrid requested cream horns at the wake, and that's when Colin made them for the first time – perfectly. Now the family get together once a year and everyone brings a dish, with Colin on cream horn duty.

COLIN'S CREAM HORNS

LON

FOOD GLORIOUS FOOD

LONDON

From Albanian and Korean to Swedish and Vietnamese, London is the place to find fantastic food from all around the world. The judges, between them, have sampled a lot of what the capital has to offer in terms of international restaurant cuisine and were hoping that this heat would give them a different taste – the home cooked, family side.

And they weren't disappointed: there were dishes from Fiji, Kenya, the Caribbean, France, Pakistan, Australia, Spain, India, Greece, South Africa ... A real United Nations of wonderful recipes.

Representing British food like mum used to make, and to the joy of all those with a soft spot for desserts, this heat also showcased some fabulous puds, including Apple Dumplings and Christmas Pudding plus some trad-with-a-twist desserts such as Rhubarb & Ginger Crumble Cheesecake and Lemon Meringue Choux Buns.

Held in the stunning landscaped grounds of Knebworth House, with the ornate turrets and towers of the house in the background, this heat gave the judges more than just great food. The diverse collection of contestants – who were from London and the surrounding counties and numbered among them a group of bikers, Hare Krishnas, a psychic, a model and a vicar – also offered Carol and our judges lessons in Cockney rhyming slang and the chance to savour chocolate-covered mealworms and locusts!

This dish reminds Jane White of her childhood in South Africa, and she was taught how to make it by her 90-year-old nanny Susie Joshua. Jane has adapted the recipe over the years to include apricot jam and extra spices. She now often cooks it for her three daughters, who always request it for dinner!

BOBOTIE & TURMERIC RICE

SERVES 5–6

2 tbsp olive oil

2 medium onions, chopped

2 garlic cloves, chopped

1 tbsp medium curry powder

1 tbsp garam masala

2 tsp ground turmeric

1 tsp ground cinnamon

2 tsp granulated sugar

pinch of chilli powder

good pinch of nutmeg

2 bay leaves

2 tbsp smooth apricot jam

2 tbsp peach or any other fruit chutney

1 Granny Smith apple, peeled and grated

1 tsp salt

½ tsp coarsely ground black pepper

500g (1lb) minced beef

2 slices of white bread

4 tbsp milk

juice of ½ lemon

50g (2oz) ground almonds

Preheat the oven to 180°C/350°F/Gas Mark 4.

Heat the oil in large saucepan and fry the onions and garlic until almost caramelised, about 5 minutes. Add the curry powder, garam masala, turmeric, cinnamon, sugar, chilli powder, nutmeg, bay leaves, apricot jam, chutney, apple, salt and pepper. Cook for 2 minutes, until fragrant. Remove from the heat and add the mince, stirring well to coat.

Put the bread and milk in a bowl, then break up the bread with a fork. Add the mixture to the mince and mix together. Stir in the lemon juice and ground almonds. Return to a medium heat and stir until heated through. Reduce the heat to low and stir constantly for 10 minutes, or until the meat is cooked. Taste for seasoning and adjust if necessary. Transfer to a casserole dish.

To prepare the topping, mix together the eggs, yoghurt, milk, salt and pepper, then pour over the curried mince in the casserole dish. Put the bay leaves on top for decoration and bake for 30 minutes, or until golden brown.

Meanwhile, prepare the rice. Bring the water to the boil with the salt and turmeric, then add the rice and stir once to separate the grains. Cover with a lid, reduce the heat to its lowest setting and cook for 15 minutes. Drain in a colander, then add the raisins, cinnamon and butter, stirring them through with a fork.

For the topping

3 eggs

125ml (4fl oz) natural yoghurt

125ml (4fl oz) milk

½ tsp salt

good pinch of coarsely ground black pepper

bay leaves

For the rice

500ml (17fl oz) water

1 tsp salt

1 tsp ground turmeric

250g (8oz) basmati rice, washed

75g (3oz) seedless raisins

1 tsp ground cinnamon

25g (1oz) butter

Bring 5cm (2in) water to the boil in a saucepan. Once boiling, reduce to a simmer, then place the colander on top of the pan. Leave to steam for no more than 10 minutes.

Serve the bobotie and rice with peach chutney and a tomato and onion salad.

CONFIT OF WINTER SPICED BELLY PORK
WITH A DUET OF VEGETABLE MOUSSES

SERVES 4

½ **side of belly pork (about 500g/1lb), scored and cleaned**

1kg (2lb) coarse salt, or enough to completely cover the belly

2 tbsp ground mixed spice

3 oranges, thickly sliced

2 large garlic bulbs, cloves separated but unpeeled

18 cloves

2 tsp peppercorns

1½ star anise, broken up

1.25–2kg (2½–4lb) goose or duck fat for covering the pork

75g (3oz) walnuts, toasted and chopped

⅓ apple, peeled, cored and finely chopped

rocket, to serve

For the orange vegetable mousse
350g (11½oz) butternut or winter squash, deseeded and chopped into 1cm (½in) dice

3 carrots, chopped into 1cm (½in) dice

Place the pork in a deep dish and rub with a handful of the salt and the mixed spice. Cover with the remaining salt, then place in the fridge for 24 hours.

The following day, preheat the oven to its lowest temperature. Place half the orange slices and half the garlic in a deep, heavy-lidded casserole dish. Add half the cloves, half the peppercorns and half the star anise. Warm gently until the fat becomes gloopy.

Brush the salt off the pork, then sit the meat on top of the garlic and orange. Add the remaining orange slices, garlic and spices. Pour the fat over the top until it's 4–5cm (1½–2in) above the pork. Cover with the lid and place in the oven for 18 hours.

Remove the casserole from the oven and set aside until completely cold. Remove the solidified fat from around the pork and cut the meat into a pleasing shape.

To serve, preheat the oven to 200°C/400°F/Gas Mark 6. Put the meat in a roasting tin and roast for 20–35 minutes, until the crackling is crisp and a rich caramel colour.

Meanwhile, make the orange mousse. Preheat the oven to 180°C/350°F/Gas Mark 4. Place all the ingredients, apart from the zest, in a roasting tin and mix thoroughly. Roast for 30 minutes, or until soft and browning. Transfer the contents of the tin to a saucepan set over a low heat. Add the orange zest and whiz with a

1 parsnip, chopped into 1cm (½in) dice

groundnut oil for coating

¼–½ tsp sesame oil (or to taste)

4 tsp honey

¼ whole nutmeg, freshly grated

1 tsp finely chopped rosemary

zest of ½ orange (or to taste)

For the white vegetable mousse
½ head of celeriac, chopped into 1cm (½in) dice

4 medium parsnips, chopped into 1cm (½in) dice

2 small turnips, chopped into 1cm (½in) dice

60ml (2½fl oz) dry sherry

4 bay leaves

3–4 tbsp double cream

¼ tsp vegetable bouillon powder

¼ tsp white pepper

salt and freshly ground black

stick blender until you have a smooth, firm consistency. Loosen with a little double cream if you wish. This mousse is best served immediately, but can be reheated later if required.

To make the white mousse, place the vegetables in a steamer set over a pan of simmering water to which you have added the sherry and bay leaves. Steam for 10–15 minutes, or until cooked. Empty the saucepan, reserving the bay leaves. Place the vegetables in the emptied pan over a low heat and whiz with a stick blender, gradually adding the cream, until you have a moderately stiff, smooth mousse. Add the bouillon powder and pepper to taste while blending. Taste and add salt if necessary. Like the orange mousse, this is best served immediately, but can be reheated later if required.

To serve the finished dish, place an 8cm (3¼in) ring mould on each plate. Place 3 tablespoons of the white mousse in each mould, then remove the ring. Place a portion of the pork on the white mousse, and put a quenelle of the orange mousse on top of that. Garnish each quenelle with a couple of rocket leaves and scatter each plate with the walnuts, apple and rocket.

Milly Wastie is the National Chair of the Federation of Young Farmers, and she cooks this hearty dish for her boyfriend after a hard day's work on the farm. Milly makes it with the beef bred on the farm and adds in organic vegetables from her father's allotment – a truly homegrown meal!

CHEESY MEATBALL PASTA

SERVES 2

300g (10oz) dried tagliatelle

1 tbsp butter

260g (8½oz) ready-made beef meatballs

2 leeks, thinly sliced

1 tsp wholegrain mustard

1 bunch of asparagus (about 8 spears), woody ends removed, or 100g (3½oz) French beans, topped and tailed

75ml (3fl oz) beef stock

150g (5oz) soft cream cheese

shavings of Parmesan cheese

freshly ground black pepper

Cook the tagliatelle in a pan of salted boiling water according to the packet instructions.

Meanwhile, melt the butter in a wok or large frying pan over a medium heat and fry the meatballs for 5 minutes, until browned on all sides. Add the leeks and fry for 2 minutes, to soften. Stir in the mustard, then add the asparagus. Pour in the stock and simmer the mixture for 5–7 minutes, until the asparagus has softened. Add the cream cheese, allow it to melt into the mixture, then stir and cook for 2 minutes.

Drain the pasta and divide between 2 plates. Top with the meatball mixture, then sprinkle with Parmesan shavings and black pepper.

Serve the pasta as it stands, or accompanied by a rocket salad and/or garlic bread.

WILD RABBIT LASAGNE
WITH SAGE-INFUSED BÉCHAMEL SAUCE

SERVES 4–6

2 young rabbits, skinned

1 large glass white wine

600ml (1 pint) chicken stock

large sprig of thyme

2 garlic cloves

½ packet (250g/8oz) of dried lasagne sheets

Parmesan cheese, freshly grated, to sprinkle

sage leaves for garnish

For the tomato sauce
olive oil

1 red onion, finely chopped

½ garlic bulb, finely chopped

2 x 400g cans of chopped tomatoes

1 bay leaf

large sprig of thyme

200g (7oz) mixed fresh wild mushrooms or 1 tbsp dried wild

Place the rabbits in a large pan, cover with the wine and stock, add the thyme and garlic, and bring to the boil. Simmer for 2–2½ hours, or until the meat is falling off the bone.

Using a slotted spoon, transfer the rabbits to a large plate. Discard the bones, then use two forks to shred the meat. Set aside.

Meanwhile, place the stock over a high heat and reduce by half.

To make the tomato sauce, heat a little oil in a pan and sauté the onion and garlic until translucent. Add the tomatoes and herbs, then simmer for 1 hour. Pour in the reduced stock and season with salt and pepper.

Preheat the oven to 180°C/350°F/Gas Mark 4.

Cook the lasagne sheets according to the packet instructions and drain well.

Meanwhile, to make the béchamel sauce, melt the butter in a saucepan and fry the chopped sage leaves in it to release their flavour. Add the flour, stirring vigorously to make a smooth paste, then gradually add the milk, stirring well between each addition. Continue stirring until the sauce has thickened, then add the Parmesan and stir to combine.

mushrooms rehydrated in 2 tbsp water for 20 minutes, not drained before use

salt and freshly ground black pepper

For the béchamel sauce
50g (2oz) butter

8–10 sage leaves, finely chopped

50g (2oz) plain flour

400ml (14fl oz) full-fat milk

125g (4oz) Parmesan cheese, freshly grated

Heat a little more olive oil in another pan and sauté the mushrooms for 5 minutes. Add the mushrooms to the tomato sauce, then stir in the shredded meat.

To assemble the dish, place half the meat mixture in the bottom of a lasagne dish. Spread half the tomato sauce over it, then cover with a layer of cooked pasta sheets. Repeat these layers once more, then cover with the béchamel sauce. Sprinkle Parmesan and sage leaves over the top and bake for 40 minutes.

Angela Wilson volunteers at a school where she teaches children with learning difficulties how to cook. Her father taught her how to cook when she was only 10 years old, and he always encouraged her to experiment with Indian food. This curry is a favourite among her family and friends, cheering them up if they feel a bit down.

CHICKEN TIKKA ON CRISPY PARATHAS
WITH CARROT & POMEGRANATE SALAD

SERVES 2

1 skinless chicken breast fillet, cut into large bite-sized pieces

2 skinless, boneless chicken thighs, cut into large bite-sized pieces

2 garlic cloves

5cm (2in) piece of fresh ginger, grated

2 green chillies, chopped

1 tsp Kashmiri chilli powder

juice and zest of 1 lemon

stalks from 1 bunch of coriander

1 medium-sized ripe mango, peeled and stoned

2 tbsp hot mango pickle

2 tbsp Greek yoghurt

Put the chicken pieces in a bowl. Place the garlic, ginger, chillies and chilli powder in a mortar and crush with a pestle to create a fine paste. Add the paste, the lemon juice and zest to the chicken and mix well. Cover and marinate in the fridge for 2 hours.

Place the coriander stalks, mango, mango pickle, yoghurt and mango powder in a blender and whiz to a fine paste. Transfer to a bowl.

Toast all the seeds and peppercorns in a dry frying pan until fragrant, then place in a mortar and crush with a pestle to a fine powder. Add to the mango mixture and stir well.

Place the chickpea flour in a dry, non-stick pan over a low heat for just a few minutes, then combine with the spiced yoghurt.

Once the chicken has marinated for 2 hours, add the yoghurt mixture and 2 tbsp of the vegetable oil. Mix well, then cover and leave overnight in the fridge.

1 tsp mango powder

¼ tsp brown mustard seeds

¼ tsp nigella seeds

½ tsp coriander seeds

¼ tsp cumin seeds

1 tsp black peppercorns

1 tbsp chickpea flour

4 tbsp vegetable oil

50g (2oz) unsalted butter

salt

For the tamarind and date chutney
1.5 litres (2½ pints) water

6 tamarind pods

6 medjool dates

pinch of black salt

pinch of chilli powder

90g (3½oz) jaggery (unrefined sugar used only for cooking)

½ tsp ground ginger

½ tsp cumin seeds

½ tsp coriander seeds

For the coriander and mint chutney
large bunch of coriander

small bunch of mint

2 garlic cloves

2 tsp lemon juice

1 green chilli

1 tsp sugar

For the salad
fleshy seeds from 1 pomegranate

2 medium carrots, cut into fine strips

¼ tsp black mustard seeds

¼ tsp nigella seeds

1 tbsp fresh lemon juice

2 tbsp honey

For the parathas
115g (3¾oz) atta (chapatti flour)

1 tbsp vegetable oil

50g (2oz) unsalted butter

Put 4 wooden skewers to soak in warm water. Remove the chicken from the fridge and bring to room temperature.

Meanwhile, make the tamarind and date chutney. Place 1 litre (1¾ pints) of the water in a saucepan, add the tamarind pods and dates and simmer for 10 minutes. Set aside to cool a little, then strain through a sieve to extract the pulp (discard everything else). Put the pulp into a saucepan, add the remaining water and bring to the boil. Add all the remaining ingredients plus a pinch of salt and simmer until thick enough to coat the back of a spoon – about 10–15 minutes. Set aside to cool.

To make the coriander and mint chutney, put all the ingredients into a blender and whiz until smooth. Add salt to taste and whiz again. Set aside until required.

To make the salad, combine the pomegranate seeds and carrots in a bowl. Toast the mustard and nigella seeds in a dry frying pan until fragrant. Remove from heat, stir in the lemon juice and honey, then add salt to taste. Once the mixture is emulsified, pour it over the pomegranate and carrots and mix well. Set aside until required.

To cook the chicken, preheat the grill until hot. Mix together the butter and remaining vegetable oil. Thread all the chicken pieces on to the skewers and place under the grill, basting regularly with the butter mixture and turning occasionally, until cooked – about 20–25 minutes.

Meanwhile, make the parathas. Put the flour into a bowl with the oil and a pinch of salt and add enough water to form a dough. Wrap the dough in cling film and set aside for 10 minutes. Cut the dough in half, roll each piece into a ball, then roll each ball into a circle about 18–20cm (7–8in) in diameter. Brush each circle with butter, then fold in half, brush with butter again and fold in half again. Roll out once more into a circle about 18–20cm (7–8in) in diameter.

Heat a dry tawa or frying pan and cook the paratha for 1 minute, until small bubbles appear, then turn over and cook the other side. Brush both sides of the paratha with a little butter, then fry for a further minute on each side. Cook the second paratha in the same way. Keep them warm until you're ready to serve.

Place the parathas on 2 serving plates, remove the chicken from the skewers, divide between parathas and spoon the carrot and pomegranate salad over. Offer the 2 chutneys in separate bowls.

CHICKEN TIKKA ON CRISPY PARATHAS

LALITHA'S
SOUTH AFRICAN
CHICKEN CURRY

SERVES 6-8

4 tbsp sunflower oil

1 medium onion, grated

2 cinnamon sticks

1 bay leaf

½ tsp fennel seeds

1 star anise

½ tbsp fresh ginger (about a 2.5cm/1 in piece), crushed

½ tbsp crushed garlic

1 heaped tbsp chilli powder

¼ tsp ground turmeric

1 tsp ground coriander

¼ tsp cumin seeds

sprig of curry leaves

breast and legs (bone in) of a medium chicken, skinned and chopped into bite-sized pieces

1 large tomato, grated

4 medium potatoes, cubed

¾ tbsp salt

1 tsp garam masala

handful of coriander, finely chopped

Warm the oil in a frying pan over a medium heat. Add the onion, cinnamon, bay leaf, fennel seeds and star anise and fry until the onion is golden brown. Add the ginger, garlic, chilli powder, turmeric, ground coriander, cumin and curry leaves and stir together.

Pour in enough water to make about 2.5cm (1in) of liquid in the pan, then add the chicken and cook for about 8 minutes. Add the tomato, potatoes and salt and cook for another 10–15 minutes. When the potatoes are soft, stir in the garam masala and chopped coriander. Serve with boiled rice.

BAKED GREEK MACARONI

Joanna Herd's Cypriot parents made this dish all the time when she was growing up in North London — it's one of the most popular dishes in Cyprus, with every family having their own take on the recipe. Joanna has adapted the version she ate in her childhood and everyone who she cooks this for says it's delicious!

SERVES 8

olive oil for frying

1 large onion, chopped

500g (1lb) minced pork

500g (1lb) minced beef

400g can of tomatoes

1 bay leaf

200ml (7fl oz) red wine

handful of flat leaf parsley, chopped

1 tbsp dried mint

1½ tsp salt

½ tsp freshly ground black pepper

2 tsp ground cinnamon

For the pasta

1 litre (1¼ pints) water

1 chicken stock cube

olive oil

250g (8oz) dried macaroni

For the béchamel sauce

125g (4oz) butter, plus extra for greasing

6 tbsp plain flour

1.5 litres (2½ pints) milk

salt

125g (4oz) halloumi cheese, grated

1 egg yolk beaten with 2 tbsp milk and a pinch of freshly grated nutmeg

Heat 1 tablespoon of olive oil in a frying pan and fry the onion until golden brown. Add the minced meat and fry, stirring frequently, until brown and the juices have evaporated. Stir in the tomatoes and bring to the boil. Add the bay leaf and simmer until almost all the liquid has evaporated. Pour in the wine and simmer again until the juices have disappeared. Add the parsley, mint, salt, pepper and cinnamon, stir well, then turn off the heat.

To prepare the pasta, put the water and stock cube in a large pan, add a drizzle of olive oil and bring to the boil. Add the macaroni and cook according to the packet instructions, or until al dente. Drain under cold running water, then stir a drizzle of olive oil through the pasta to prevent sticking.

To make the béchamel sauce, melt the butter in a non-stick pan, then stir in the flour until smooth. Gradually add the milk, stirring between each addition. Add a little salt and the halloumi and continue stirring until the cheese has melted. Take the sauce off the heat and stir in the egg mixture. Add a little extra milk if it seems too thick. Return to the heat, stirring constantly until the first bubbles appear on the surface, then remove from the heat.

Butter a large ovenproof dish and add one-third of the macaroni. Spoon half the mince mixture over it, then pour a very thin layer of the béchamel over that. Add another third of the macaroni, spoon the remaining mince over it, and cover with the rest of the macaroni. Pour the remaining béchamel over the surface and set aside to cool for at least 1 hour.

Preheat the oven to 180°C/350°F/Gas Mark 4.

Bake the macaroni for 35–45 minutes until bubbling and lightly browned, then set aside to rest for at least 10–15 minutes before serving. The dish is equally good hot or cold.

The yoghurt and ground almonds in Sophia Graham's sponges mean that they freeze well, keeping their flavour. Sophia loves to experiment with sponges and cakes, and once a week cooks with the produce from the garden at Holly Lodge in Richmond, where she volunteers, teaching disabled children how to grow plants.

SOPHIE'S APPLE, BLACKBERRY & YOGHURT SPONGE PUDDINGS

MAKES ABOUT 9

90g (3½oz) unsalted butter, plus extra for greasing

135g (4½oz) icing sugar

2 large eggs, separated

90g (3½oz) Greek yoghurt

1 heaped tsp orange zest

1 tsp vanilla extract

2 tbsp ground almonds

1 tsp baking powder

115g (3¾oz) self-raising flour

about 18 frozen blackberries

For the custard

125g (4oz) ground almonds

500ml (17fl oz) full-fat milk

5 large egg yolks

2 tbsp caster sugar

200ml (7fl oz) double cream

freshly grated nutmeg

2 cloves

The day before you want to serve the puddings, place the ground almonds and milk for the custard together in a jug and leave in the fridge overnight.

To make the pudding, first prepare the apples. Melt the butter in a pan with the caster sugar. Add the apples and cook for 5 minutes. Stir in the honey, then set aside.

Preheat the oven to 160°C/325°F/Gas Mark 3 and butter 9 small ramekins (the number depends on the size of the dishes).

To make the sponge batter, beat the butter and icing sugar until light and fluffy. Add the egg yolks and yoghurt, mix well, then add the orange zest and vanilla extract.

Combine the ground almonds, baking powder and flour in a bowl, then gradually add them to the butter mixture.

Whisk the egg whites until they form stiff peaks. Carefully fold them into the butter mixture a third at a time.

Place a tablespoon of the cooked apples in the bottom of each prepared ramekin, then pour in enough of the batter to ensure each dish is three-quarters full. Top each one with 2 frozen blackberries, then place the dishes in a deep roasting tin. Slide the tin into a multi-purpose roasting bag and pour enough boiling water into the tin to come halfway up the side of the ramekins. Seal the bag and place in the oven for 25 minutes, or until the puddings have risen well and the mixture is pulling away from the sides of the dishes.

For the apples

25g (1oz) unsalted butter

2 tbsp caster sugar

5 Golden Delicious apples, peeled, cored and chopped

3 tbsp runny honey

For the compote

165g (5½oz) frozen blackberries

35g (1¼oz) white sugar

3 tbsp water

1 tsp arrowroot

1 tbsp black raspberry liqueur, such as Chambord (optional)

To finish making the custard, put the egg yolks and sugar in a bowl and beat together until light in colour. Put the chilled almond and milk mixture into a pan with the double cream and warm through. Add the egg yolk mixture, then stir in nutmeg to taste and the cloves. Continue heating gently, stirring constantly, until the custard thickens enough to coat the back of a spoon. Cover and keep warm until ready to serve.

To prepare the compote, set aside about 27 of the blackberries (3 per person), keeping them frozen. Dissolve the sugar in a small pan with the water. Add the remaining blackberries and cook over a high heat until they have reduced to a pulp. Pass through a sieve, discarding the seeds, then stir in the arrowroot. Add the raspberry liqueur (if using), then drop in the reserved blackberries, stir lightly and set aside.

Invert each pudding onto a plate, drizzle a little custard around it and top with the compote. Serve the remaining custard in a jug for people to help themselves.

Returning from the Navy on leave, Tony Appleton suggested to his mother that she add some dark Navy Rum to the traditional family bread and butter pudding recipe, passed down from his great grandmother. The family have never looked back, and now Tony makes it at least 4 times a month using Pusser's British Navy Rum from the Virgin Islands.

BREAD & BUTTER PUDDING

SERVES 4

115g (3¾oz) dried fruit

3 tbsp good-quality dark rum, such as Pusser's Rum

butter

4–6 slices white sliced bread, crusts removed

marmalade

zest of 1 orange

zest of 1 lemon

75g (3oz) brown sugar

3 large eggs

600ml (1 pint) milk

Put the fruit and rum in a bowl and leave to soak for 1 hour.

Butter an ovenproof dish 22 x 22 x 5cm (8½ x 8½ x 2in). Drain the soaked fruit.

Butter the bread, then spread each slice with marmalade. Cut each slice into 4 triangles. Place a single layer of the triangles in the prepared dish. Sprinkle with one-third of the zests, sugar and fruit. Repeat this step twice more to give 3 layers in total.

Beat the eggs and add the milk. Pour the mixture over the bread and allow to soak for 1 hour.

Preheat the oven to 150°C/300°F/Gas Mark 2, then bake the pudding on the middle shelf for 1 hour.

Serve with double cream.

This dish is special to Elaine Dennington because it relates to both of her grandmothers. Her French grandmother had six children to feed, so created an inexpensive pudding using homegrown apples. Elaine's English grandmother made mulberry jelly every autumn from the tree in her garden. Elaine put the two together and hey presto!

BAKED APPLE DUMPLINGS

WITH MULBERRY JELLY

**SERVES 2 AND MAKES
ABOUT 2 LITRES
(3½ PINTS) JELLY**

1 tsp ground cinnamon

50g (2oz) soft brown sugar

**2 medium Bramley apples, peeled
and cored, but kept whole**

**1 tbsp granulated sugar for
sprinkling**

For the mulberry jelly
1 lemon, quartered

**6 cooking apples, roughly
chopped (skin on and seeds in)**

1kg (2lb) mulberries

1.2 litres (2 pints) water

**about 500g (1lb) granulated sugar
(the amount of sugar will depend
on the amount of juice the fruit
yields – you need 500g/1lb per
600ml/1 pint of juice)**

First make the jelly. Put the lemon, apples and mulberries in a large saucepan with the water, bring to the boil, then simmer for 30 minutes, or until the apples fall apart. Pour the mixture into a jelly bag suspended over a basin and leave to strain overnight. Do not squeeze the bag or the jelly will be cloudy.

Discard the pulp and measure the juice into a large pan, then add 500g (1lb) sugar per 600ml (1 pint). Bring to the boil, stirring constantly, then simmer for 30 minutes, until the mixture registers 108°C/226°F on a sugar thermometer, or until a spoonful of it placed on a very cold plate forms a skin that wrinkles when pushed. When you have reached this stage, pour the jelly into a warm sterilised jar (see Tip, page 57), cover with a waxed disk and set aside to cool.

To make the pastry, put all the dry ingredients into a bowl and rub in the margarine with your fingertips until the mixture resembles breadcrumbs. Add the water a bit at a time until a dough forms. Wrap in cling film and place in the fridge for at least 30 minutes.

Preheat the oven to 180°C/350°F/Gas Mark 4.

Combine the cinnamon and brown sugar on a plate and roll the apples in it to coat them thoroughly.

For the pastry
175g (6oz) plain flour, plus extra for dusting

½ tsp baking powder

pinch of salt

75g (3oz) soft margarine

about 75ml (3fl oz) water

Cut the chilled pastry in half. On a lightly floured work surface, roll each half into a circle about 5mm (¼in) thick and large enough to wrap around each fruit. Place an apple on each circle, flattest end down, and spoon the jelly into the cored middle. Gather the pastry at the top of the apple and seal the edges together with water. Place on a baking sheet, sealed side down, then brush with water and sprinkle with the granulated sugar. Stab the top of the apple parcels with a sharp knife to allow steam to escape. If you have any leftover pastry, cut out some leaf shapes and stick them to the dumpling with water.

Bake for 10 minutes, then lower the heat to 150°C/300°F/Gas Mark 2 and bake for a further 30 minutes, until the pastry is golden and a skewer can be pushed easily through the centre.

Serve with custard, clotted cream or ice cream.

Ellie McCausland developed a love for food and cooking when she worked as a waitress — and fell for the chef! She now cooks the meals at home in between studying for her PhD, and developed this recipe because it combines quintessentially British rhubarb with her two favourite desserts — cheesecake and crumble.

ELLIE'S RHUBARB & GINGER CRUMBLE CHEESECAKE

SERVES 8-10

- 400g (13oz) rhubarb, cut into 2.5cm (1in) pieces
- 50g (2oz) caster sugar
- 3 tbsp water
- drop of red food colouring (optional)
- 1 tsp arrowroot mixed with 2 tsp cold water
- 375g (12oz) ricotta cheese
- 300ml (½ pint) half-fat crème fraîche
- 1½ tbsp runny honey
- 125g (4oz) caster sugar
- 3 large eggs
- 1 tsp vanilla extract
- sprigs of mint, to decorate

Preheat the oven to 190°C/375°F/Gas Mark 5. Butter a shallow 20cm (8in) springform cake tin.

Put the rhubarb into a baking dish with the sugar and water, toss together and bake for 25–40 minutes, depending on the thickness of the rhubarb, until tender.

Meanwhile, make the base. Melt the butter in a small saucepan, then mix in the crushed biscuits. Tip the mixture into the prepared tin and press it down evenly with the back of a spoon. Brush with the egg white and bake for 10 minutes, until golden and firm. Set aside to cool.

Mash the cooked rhubarb to a purée with a fork. Drain well, then add the food colouring (if using). Pour in the arrowroot mixture and stir to thicken. Set aside to cool.

Put the ricotta, crème fraîche, honey, sugar, eggs and vanilla extract in a blender or food processor and whiz until combined. Transfer to a bowl and swirl the rhubarb purée through it with a fork. Don't overmix - the idea is to create pink streaks.

For the base
65g (2½oz) butter, plus extra for greasing

18 gingernut biscuits, crushed

1 egg white

For the crumble
90g (3½oz) wholemeal flour

40g (1½oz) cold butter, cubed

40g (1½oz) demerara sugar

1 tsp ground ginger

50g (2oz) blanched almonds, roughly chopped

1 tbsp cold water

Reduce the oven temperature to 180°C/350°F/Gas Mark 4 and put an empty roasting tin in the bottom of it.

Butter the sides of the cake tin again, then pour the ricotta mixture over the biscuit base. Cover the tin tightly with foil, then place in the oven and quickly pour a jug of cold water into the empty roasting tin. Close the oven door and bake for 30 minutes.

Meanwhile, make the crumble. Put the flour and butter in a bowl and rub together until the mixture resembles fine breadcrumbs. Stir in the sugar, ginger and almonds, then gently stir in the water to form small 'pebbles' in the mixture.

Remove the cheesecake from the oven, discard the foil and spread the crumble mixture over the top of the cake. Remove the tray of water from the oven and increase the temperature to 190°C/375°F/Gas Mark 5. Bake the cheesecake for a further 30 minutes, until a skewer inserted in the middle comes out clean. Set aside until cool, then refrigerate until needed. Remember to bring it back to room temperature 30 minutes before serving: no one wants cold crumble. Decorate with mint sprigs.

Police officer Samantha Egan loves chocolate and loves baking, and this is her favourite combination of both. The brownies are perfect with a cup of tea or can be elevated to a dinner party dessert by serving with the vanilla-flavoured clotted cream.

DOUBLE CHOCOLATE GANACHE BROWNIES
WITH VANILLA CLOTTED CREAM

SERVES 9

135g (4½oz) dark chocolate

125g (4oz) unsalted butter, plus extra for greasing

200g (7oz) golden caster sugar

2 large eggs

1 vanilla pod, split open lengthways and seeds scraped out

80g (3¼oz) plain flour

1 heaped tbsp cocoa powder

pinch of salt

25g (1oz) white chocolate chunks

25g (1oz) milk chocolate chunks

25g (1oz) dark chocolate chunks

Preheat the oven to 160°C/325°F/Gas Mark 3. Butter a 20cm (8in) square baking tin and line it with baking parchment.

Melt the dark chocolate and butter in a bowl placed over a saucepan of simmering water. Give it a good mix to ensure all the chocolate has melted, then remove from the heat and stir in the sugar. Leave for 5 minutes to cool a little.

In a separate bowl, beat the eggs with the vanilla seeds. Add this mixture to the chocolate a bit at a time, beating well after each addition. Sift in the flour, cocoa and salt and fold together. Finally, stir in the chocolate chunks, distributing them as evenly as possible.

Pour the mixture into the prepared tin and bake for about 20 minutes, until the sponge springs back when lightly pressed with a finger, or a skewer inserted in the middle comes out clean. Set aside to cool in the tin for 10 minutes, then turn on to a wire rack to cool.

For the ganache
150g (5oz) milk chocolate, broken into pieces

150ml (¼ pint) double cream

25g (1oz) unsalted butter

For the clotted cream
300ml (½ pint) double cream

1 vanilla pod, split open lengthways and seeds scraped out

To make the ganache, put the chocolate and cream in a heatproof bowl set over a saucepan of simmering water. Once the chocolate has melted, give it a good mix, then remove from the heat and add the butter, mixing until smooth. Set aside to cool to room temperature.

Spread the ganache over the brownie sponge, then place in the fridge to set for at least a couple of hours.

To prepare the cream, preheat the oven to 120°C/250°F/Gas Mark ½. Combine the cream and vanilla seeds, then pour into a small roasting tin and place in the oven for 40 minutes. Strain the cream into a bowl, discarding any bits left in the sieve, then pour into shot glasses and leave to set in the fridge for a few hours.

To serve, cut the brownie sponge into 9 squares and serve with the clotted cream.

This summer cake is a dreamy combination of sponge, meringue, strawberries and cream — and is loved by all who taste it. Mandy Maloney was given the recipe by her mother over 20 years ago, and hopes that she'll be passing it on to her own daughter, who is already a keen cook.

STRAWBERRY SPONGE MERINGUE CAKE

SERVES 12

50g (2oz) butter, plus extra for greasing

115g (3¾oz) caster sugar

4 egg yolks

125g (4oz) self-raising flour

5 tbsp full-fat milk

1 tsp vanilla extract

90g (3½oz) white chocolate

200g (7oz) ripe strawberries, hulled and sliced, plus 8 whole strawberries

For the meringue topping

4 egg whites

pinch of salt

225g (7½oz) caster sugar

25g (1oz) flaked almonds, to decorate

For the filling

300ml (½ pint) double cream

dash of sherry

1 tbsp caster sugar

Preheat the oven to 150°C/300°F/Gas Mark 2. Butter two 23cm (9in) round cake tins and line them with baking parchment.

Put the butter and sugar in a bowl and cream together until light and fluffy. Beat in the egg yolks one at a time. Gradually fold in the flour, milk and vanilla extract, alternating between dry and wet ingredients. Divide the mixture equally between the prepared tins (it is much thinner than a normal sponge cake) and set aside.

To make the meringue, put the egg whites into a clean bowl, add the salt and whisk until stiff peaks form. Gradually beat in the sugar, then spread half the meringue over each tin of sponge mixture. Use a spatula or a fork to make attractive swirls or peaks. Sprinkle one cake with flaked almonds (this will be the top layer).

Bake the cakes for about 45 minutes, until a skewer inserted through both meringue and sponge comes out clean. Carefully remove from the tins and cool on a wire rack.

To make the filling, whip the cream with the sherry and sugar until soft peaks form.

Place the white chocolate in a bowl and heat in the microwave for 1 minute, or until it has completely melted, checking and stirring every 20 seconds. Half-dip the whole strawberries in the chocolate and place on a sheet of greaseproof paper to set.

When the cakes have cooled, put three-quarters of the cream filling on the base sponge, arrange the strawberry slices over it, then sit the flaked almond sponge on top. Place the remaining cream filling in a piping bag fitted with a star-shaped nozzle and pipe 8 small swirls on top of the cake. Top each swirl with a chocolate-dipped strawberry.

MIDLANDS

THE MIDLANDS

It was Wales versus the Midlands at this heat at the Three Counties Showground during the Malvern Autumn Show.

The Welsh turned out in force, complete with a busload of schoolchildren laden with wares to be sampled. And what a variety the Welsh contestants provided: among them were the fruity teatime Welsh Cakes, several family recipes for Cawl – widely considered to be the national dish of Wales – plus delicious recipes that made full use of Wales's fabulous cheeses, such as Merthyr Sausages and a Savoury Bread & Butter Pudding.

In the Midlands' corner we had many regional specialities, including Staffordshire Oatcakes, Shropshire Fidget Pie, a Rarebit laced with a dash of local Worcestershire Sauce, and a delectable variation on Bakewell Tart. The story goes that the Bakewell Tart was invented by accident in 1860 at the Rutland Arms in Bakewell, Derbyshire, when an inexperienced kitchen maid got the recipe for jam tart wrong. The story is probably apochryphal, but, no matter, the end result is a firm favourite around the whole country.

The day was full of lots of other wonderful flavours and surprises: a best-of-British jelly made with Pimm's, an historical recipe given to us by a mother and son who live – and cook – as the Victorians did, and an unexpected invasion of ducks in the *Food Glorious Food* tent!

Following heart surgery in 2010, Barnaby Reid is on medication that leaves a metallic taste in his mouth, so he has been exploring what kind of foods will taste best with the help of his mum, Fiona. Together they tried all kinds of egg dishes on an 'Eggy Tour of the World', and this recipe is Barnaby's own invention that his mum cooks for him – with a little help in the kitchen from her son, of course.

EGGS BARNABY

SERVES 1

50g (2oz) broccoli, cut into small florets

1 English muffin, halved and lightly toasted

2 slices of honey roast ham

For the cheese sauce
4 tbsp butter

4 tbsp plain flour

8 tbsp milk

25g (1oz) mature Cheddar cheese, grated, plus extra for sprinkling

pinch of mustard powder

salt and freshly ground black pepper

For the eggs
dash of vinegar

pinch of salt

2 eggs (the fresher, the better)

Steam the broccoli for 6–7 minutes, or until tender.

To make the sauce, melt the butter in a pan, stir in the flour and cook for just under a minute. Whisk in the milk a bit at a time to avoid lumps forming, then bring to the boil, stirring continuously. Cook for 2 minutes, then take off the heat, add the cheese and mustard powder and season to taste.

To cook the eggs, half-fill a saucepan with water, add the vinegar and salt and bring to a gentle simmer. Stir the water vigorously with a balloon whisk to create a whirlpool and crack an egg into the centre. Reduce the heat to low, and cook for 5 minutes. Remove from the water with a slotted spoon, drain on kitchen paper and keep warm. Repeat with the second egg.

Place the muffin halves on a serving plate. Put a slice of ham, a poached egg and half the broccoli on each one, then top with the cheese sauce. Serve straight away, sprinkled with a little extra grated cheese and a twist of pepper if liked.

Theo Theobald brought this dish into being when his kids were small and the cupboards were bare. The 'wobbly' element comes about when you add whatever comes to hand – Theo has made it to include all kinds of ingredients from turmeric to truffles. The only ingredient never to be omitted is the Worcestershire sauce!

WOBBLY WORCESTER RAREBIT

SERVES 1, BUT ALSO MAKES A 500G (1LB) LOAF

2 thick slices of homemade tomato bread (see below), or other good-quality bread

1 egg

½ tsp Worcestershire sauce

2 small garlic cloves, finely chopped

1 tsp French wholegrain mustard

75g (3oz) mature Cheddar cheese, grated

50g (2oz) Gruyère cheese, grated

1 tsp finely chopped chives (optional)

1 spring onion, finely sliced (optional)

parsley for garnish

For the tomato bread (optional)
300ml (10fl oz) tepid water

500g (1lb) strong white bread flour

2 tbsp milk powder

1 tbsp caster sugar

1 tsp bread-machine yeast or fast-action yeast if not using a machine

35g (1¼oz) butter

8 sun-dried tomatoes, very finely chopped

1½ tsp salt

1 tbsp tomato purée

If making the bread in a bread-maker, combine all the ingredients in it and use the 'basic' setting, selecting a light crust if you have that option. It is important to use exact quantities and add the ingredients in the order they are listed, otherwise it can all go horribly wrong.

If making the bread by hand, lightly grease a large loaf tin lightly with butter. Place the flour, milk powder, sugar, yeast and salt in a large bowl and mix together. Add the tepid water, followed by the butter, sun-dried tomatoes and tomato paste and mix until it has come together. Lightly flour a work surface, then turn the dough and knead for 10 minutes. Put the dough in a clean bowl, cover with a tea towel and place somewhere warm for 45 minutes or until doubled in volume. Return the dough to a floured work surface and knock back the dough. Then transfer to a covered bowl as before, and leave for 30 minutes. Knock back once more and form into a smooth loaf shape (the size of your loaf tin) and place in the tin. Cover and leave to prove for 30 minutes, preheating the oven to 200°C/400°F/Gas Mark 6 about 10 minutes before the dough is ready. Place in the oven and bake for 30–35 minutes. To check that it is cooked, tap the base of the bread with your fingers – if it sounds hollow the bread is ready.

Turn out of the bread maker or tin and place on a wire rack for 1½ hours until cooled completely.

Lightly toast the bread slices under a grill. Meanwhile, beat the egg in a bowl, then mix in the Worcestershire sauce, garlic and mustard. Add the grated cheese, chives and spring onions (if using), then spread on the toast, right to the edges, using the back of a spoon. Place under the hot grill until the rarebit has a browny-yellow glaze. Garnish with parsley and eat straight away.

MERTHYR SAUSAGES
WITH PLUM CHUTNEY

SERVES 4

115g (3¾oz) fresh brown breadcrumbs

125g (4oz) Caerphilly cheese, grated

2 small leeks, finely chopped

2 tbsp chopped thyme leaves

1 tsp lemon zest

1 tsp mustard powder

75g (3oz) goats' cheese, coarsely chopped

2 eggs, 1 separated

1 tbsp milk

salt and freshly ground black pepper

50g (2oz) plain flour

2 tbsp fresh white breadcrumbs

2 tbsp sunflower oil

shredded sage leaves for garnish

For the chutney

250g (8oz) plums, stoned and quartered

4 tbsp balsamic vinegar

2 tbsp soft brown sugar

1 garlic clove, minced

¼ tsp freshly grated ginger

First make the chutney. Put all the ingredients for it in a saucepan and bring to the boil over a medium heat, stirring constantly. Simmer until the mixture thickens, then remove from the heat and set aside to cool.

To make the sausages, put the brown breadcrumbs, Caerphilly, leeks, thyme, lemon zest and mustard powder in a bowl. Gradually beat the goats' cheese into the mixture.

Add the egg plus the separated egg yolk and milk to the cheese mixture and beat together. Season to taste.

Divide the mixture into 8 equal pieces and roll into sausages about 7.5cm (3in) long. Cover and chill for 1 hour to allow the flavour to develop.

Combine the flour and white breadcrumbs on a plate. Brush the chilled sausages with the egg white, then coat them lightly in the flour mixture.

Heat the oil in a frying pan, add the sausages and cook over a medium heat for 8–10 minutes, turning regularly, until golden brown. Drain on kitchen paper to soak up any excess oil, then garnish with the sage and serve at once with the plum chutney.

Morgan Lewis was spurred on to do more cooking when he reached the semi-finals of a school cookery competition. He loves the combination of ingredients in these meat-free sausages because the Welsh goats' cheese he uses adds a great flavour, which goes really well with the chutney.

DRAGON'S PIE

SERVES 4-6

8 small leeks (about 600g/ 1lb 2oz), cut in half widthways

10 medium potatoes, quartered

50g (2oz) butter or margarine

8 thick slices of smoked ham, cut in half to make 16 strips

200g (7oz) hot chilli Cheddar cheese, such as Dragon's Breath Cheddar cheese, thinly sliced

For the cheese sauce
65g (2½oz) butter or margarine

salt and freshly ground pepper

65g (2½oz) plain flour

500ml (17fl oz) milk

200g (7oz) mature Cheddar cheese, such as Pwll Mawr Cheddar cheese, crumbled

1 tsp Worcestershire sauce

Preheat the oven to 200°C/400°F/Gas Mark 6.

First make the sauce. Put a saucepan over a medium-low heat, add the butter plus a pinch of salt and pepper and melt slowly. Add the flour, whisk until well combined, then cook for 2 minutes. Take the pan off the heat and slowly add a quarter of the milk, whisking until smooth. Return the pan to the heat, add another quarter of the milk and whisk again. Increase the heat to medium-high, add the remaining milk and heat for 1–2 minutes, until beginning to thicken. Add the Pwll Mawr cheese, stir until thick and creamy, then mix in the Worcestershire sauce. Set aside.

Place the leeks in a saucepan with just enough water to cover them. Bring to the boil over a medium-high heat, then simmer for about 5 minutes, until starting to soften. Drain, then place on a clean tea towel to cool and dry.

Put the potatoes in a saucepan of salted water, bring to the boil, then simmer for 15–20 minutes, until just soft enough to mash. Drain, add the butter and mash the potatoes until light and fluffy. Season to taste.

Wrap each cooled leek in a strip of ham and place in a large ovenproof dish (about 20 x 15 x 15cm/8 x 6 x 6in). Cover them with the cheese sauce, then smooth the mashed potato over the top. Sprinkle with the Dragon's Breath Cheddar and place in the oven for 20–25 minutes, until the pie is thoroughly hot in the middle and golden brown on top. Serve with crusty bread.

Paul Jarratt developed this recipe after eating a regional Portuguese dish on holiday that had similar flavours. Paul cooks for his mum once a week, and has a cook-off competition with his mate twice a month, where he's usually declared the winner!

FILLET OF PORK WRAPPED IN BLACK FOREST HAM
WITH ROASTED VEG & REDCURRANT JUS

SERVES 2

2 large potatoes

6 tbsp olive oil

2 garlic cloves, bashed

5 sprigs of thyme

15g (½oz) butter

400g (13oz) fillet of pork tenderloin

½ tsp dried mixed herbs

5 slices of Black Forest ham

2–3 fresh figs, quartered

1 tbsp maple syrup

8 asparagus spears

pinch of freshly grated nutmeg

Preheat the oven to 200°C/400°F/Gas Mark 6.

First make the jus. Place all the ingredients for it in a small saucepan and heat gently for 10–15 minutes, or until the liquid coats the back of a spoon. Keep warm.

Cut two 2.5cm (1in) thick slices from the middle of each potato and trim them into neat rectangles. Cook in a pan of boiling water for 7 minutes, then drain.

Heat half the olive oil in an ovenproof frying pan, add the garlic and thyme and allow to infuse for 3 minutes. Discard the garlic and thyme, add the potatoes and half the butter, season well and fry over a medium heat until golden brown on both sides. Transfer to the oven for 10 minutes, until the potatoes are cooked through and have darkened slightly.

Season the pork with black pepper and the mixed herbs, then rub with 1 tablespoon of the olive oil. Arrange the ham slices side by side on a chopping board, overlapping them slightly. Place the pork fillet along the bottom edge of the slices and roll the ham around it reasonably tightly.

For the jus

juice of 1 large orange

2 tbsp redcurrant jelly

2 tbsp port

½ tsp demerara sugar

1 cinnamon stick

salt and freshly ground black pepper

Heat 1 tablespoon of the olive oil and the remaining butter in a large, ovenproof frying pan, add the encased fillet and cook on a medium-high heat for 5–6 minutes, or until the ham has browned all over. Transfer to the oven for 7–8 minutes, then check if the meat is cooked by inserting a skewer or sharp knife into the thickest part for 8 seconds, then placing it against the back of your hand – if the metal is hot, remove the meat from the oven, cover with foil and set aside to rest for 5 minutes.

While the meat is cooking, line a large baking sheet with foil. Add the figs, drizzle with maple syrup and season to taste, then add the asparagus, season to taste and drizzle with the remaining olive oil. Place in the oven for 10 minutes, until the figs are starting to caramelise but the asparagus is still very slightly firm.

To serve, slice the rested pork into medallions about 2.5cm (1in) thick. Pour some of the jus on to 2 serving plates, arrange the potatoes, pork, figs and asparagus on it, then drizzle with the remaining jus. Sprinkle with the nutmeg, season with pepper and serve immediately.

Trish MacCurrach discovered the Serbian way of cooking outdoors on a Kotlich when she joined her husband, who was part of the post-war disaster relief programme, in Serbia. This dish uses seasonal, local produce with a Serbian twist, and is best cooked outside over a fire, but will still taste great made in the kitchen.

PHEASANT PAPRIKASH

SERVES 6

olive oil

1 large onion, finely chopped

5 garlic cloves, chopped

4 pheasant breasts (about 125g/4oz each)

400g can of tomatoes, each tomato chopped into 2–3 pieces

200g (7oz) cooked chestnuts

225g (7½oz) kiseli kupus or sauerkraut

400g (13oz) precooked ham hock, chopped into chunks

3–4 medium potatoes, roughly chopped

500ml (17fl oz) water

½ tsp chilli flakes

¼ tsp cumin seeds

3 fresh bay leaves

sprig of rosemary

4 tsp sweet paprika

salt and freshly ground black pepper

Heat the oil in a large frying pan and fry the onion and garlic until transparent.

Chop each pheasant breast into 3 long pieces and fry with the onion mixture until slightly brown – about 3 minutes on each side. Add the remaining ingredients with half the paprika plus some salt and pepper. Simmer for 20–30 minutes, stirring occasionally to prevent sticking.

Add the remaining paprika when the potatoes are soft to the point of a sharp knife. Taste and adjust the seasoning if necessary, then take off the heat and rest for 5 minutes.

Serve with dollops of sour cream, a sprinkling of chopped parsley and chunks of crusty bread.

CAWL

SERVES 8–10

1kg (2lb) best-end neck of lamb, whole

1.8 litres (3 pints) water

salt and freshly ground black pepper

2 large onions, sliced

3 celery sticks, including leaves, thinly sliced

4 medium carrots, thickly sliced

1 large parsnip, cut into 2.5cm (1in) chunks

1 medium swede, cut into 2.5cm (1in) chunks

3 leeks, sliced

bunch of parsley, chopped

4 medium potatoes, cut into 2.5cm (1in) chunks

Put the lamb and water into a very large saucepan and add seasoning. Bring to the boil, then simmer gently for 1 hour. Set aside to cool, then place in the fridge overnight. The next day, skim the fat off the surface, lift out the lamb and take the meat off the bone – it should come away easily. Shred the meat with two forks, then return it to the pan. (If you don't have time to leave the lamb overnight, skim the fat off while it is simmering, then shred the meat and return it to the pan as described.)

Add the onions, celery, carrots, parsnip, swede, two-thirds of the leeks and half the parsley. Cover and simmer for 1 hour.

Add the potatoes and cook for 10 minutes. Add the remaining leek and cook for a further 10 minutes. Stir in the remaining parsley and taste for seasoning. Serve with soda bread and Caerphilly cheese.

This traditional Welsh dish has been passed down the generations of Sian Day's family. She got the recipe from her grandfather, who used to cook the dish every week. It's best to prepare the meat in advance, though the dish will still be delicious if you don't have time.

NEIL'S FAGGITS AN PAYS

SERVES 5

350g (11½oz) pig's heart

350g (11½oz) pig's liver

350g (11½oz) pig's kidney

350g (11½oz) pig's lights (lungs)

115g (3¾oz) dried white
breadcrumbs

1 medium onion, finely chopped

1½ tbsp finely chopped sage

salt and freshly ground black
pepper

1½ tbsp plain flour for dusting

1½ tsp sunflower oil for greasing

5 large potatoes, cut in half

For the peas
300g (10oz) dried marrowfat peas

1 tbsp bicarbonate of soda

For the gravy
600ml (1 pint) water

1 tbsp cornflour mixed with 4 tbsp
cold water

2 tbsp gravy browning

1 tsp English mustard (optional)

First prepare the peas. Place them in a bowl with the bicarbonate of soda, cover with water and leave to soak overnight.

Preheat the oven to 180°C/350°F/Gas Mark 4. Oil a 28 x 20cm (11 x 8in) baking dish.

Trim all the veins, sinew and fat from the offal and set aside for the gravy. Weigh what is left – you should have about 225g (7½oz) of each type. Place them separately in a blender or food processor and pulse until broken up but not liquidised. Transfer to a mixing bowl and add the breadcrumbs, onion and sage. Season well.

With floured hands, take handfuls of the mixture and shape into 5 large balls or 10 small ones. Make sure each ball is tightly packed.

Put the flour on a plate and roll each faggot in it, then place them in the fridge for at least 30 minutes.

Put the chilled faggots into the prepared baking dish and pour in enough water to come three-quarters of the way up them. Cover the dish with foil and bake for 45 minutes. Remove the foil and bake for a further 1½ hours, checking the water every 15–20 minutes and topping it up to maintain a constant level. With 20 minutes to go, stop topping up the water and allow most of it to evaporate. By the end of the cooking time, the faggots will be slightly crisp and firm.

Drain the peas, rinse them in cold water and place in a steamer over a medium heat for 30–60 minutes. The longer the peas are steamed for, the mushier they will be.

With 40 minutes of faggot cooking time left, put the potatoes on to boil for 20–30 minutes, depending on how firm you like them. I like mine soft so that they can be mashed up with the gravy and the peas.

Originally from Dudley in the Midlands, Neil Brookes was brought up on cheap and nutritious Black Country dishes such as this one, which is otherwise known as Faggots and Peas. Everyone he makes this traditional dish for loves it, and he'll quite often make a big vat of it on a Sunday and still be enjoying it on Wednesday!

To make the gravy, put the reserved offal trimmings and water into a large pan and bring to the boil. Simmer for 30 minutes, then strain through a sieve, discarding all the solids. Return the stock to the pan (there should be about 450ml/¾ pint) and bring to the boil. Slowly add the cornflour mixture, stirring until the desired thickness is reached. Add the gravy browning and the mustard (if using), then season to taste.

Transfer the faggots to a warmed plate, cover with a clean tea towel and keep warm. Pour any juices from the baking dish into the gravy, stirring as it comes to the boil, and continue bubbling until reduced to about 300ml (½ pint).

To serve, divide the boiled potatoes between 5 warmed serving plates, place the faggots alongside and add a good helping of mushy peas. Spoon some gravy all over and serve with thick slices of crusty bread.

Staffordshire oatcakes are a sort of pancake, and DJ and radio presenter Terry Bossons loves the regional delicacy so much that he started Oatcake Day in 2010. The Facebook group has over 8,000 members, and Titanic Breweries, based in Stoke-on-Trent, has even been inspired to make an oatcake ale!

TERRY'S STAFFORDSHIRE OATCAKES

MAKES 6

250g (8oz) oatmeal

150g (5oz) plain flour

1 tsp salt

1 litre (1¾ pints) hot water

14g sachet of dried yeast

3 tsp baking powder

2 tsp bicarbonate of soda

freshly ground black pepper

olive oil for frying

6 rashers of bacon

brown sauce, to taste

250g (8oz) Cheddar cheese, grated

6 small strings of cherry tomatoes on the vine

Combine the oatmeal, flour and salt in a bowl. Add 300ml (½ pint) of the hot water and mix until smooth. Add the yeast and give it another stir. Gradually add more water, stirring until incorporated and the consistency is similar to lumpy pancake batter. Add the baking powder, bicarbonate of soda and a pinch of pepper, then cover with a large container or tea towel and leave to stand for 1 hour.

Preheat the oven to 180°C/350°C/Gas Mark 4.

Heat a little oil in a frying pan until very hot. Add a ladleful of the batter and cook for about 1 minute, until bubbles start to form (the oatcake should be about 20cm/8in in diameter). Flip over using a fish slice, and fry for 1 minute on the other side, or until brown and dry. Transfer to a baking sheet while you make another 5 oatcakes.

Fry the bacon until crisp and divide it equally between the oatcakes, placing it on the bottom half of each one. Drizzle with the brown sauce, then fold the oatcakes in half, sprinkle with the cheese and place in the oven for 5 minutes, or until the cheese has melted.

Meanwhile, heat a little olive oil in a pan over a low heat, add the tomatoes and cook for about 5 minutes.

Serve the oatcakes garnished with the tomatoes.

Tammy Holmes is restaurant manager for Wiggly Worm at Star Bistro, the restaurant at National Star College for young people with disabilities. The recipe was originally a red wine jelly from Matt, the chef. Joe and Tristan suggested he change the red wine to Pimm's; Sara and Rachel decided on which fruits should be used in the jelly; and Georgina, Colin, Shantelle and Oscar wrote up the recipe. This dish is the first one the group has created together.

STAR PIMM'S FRUIT JELLY

SERVES 9

450g (14½oz) mixed berries, plus extra to garnish

3 mint leaves, finely chopped, plus extra to garnish

150ml (¼ pint) Pimm's No. 1

7 gelatine leaves

600ml (1 pint) sparkling wine, such as Three Choirs sparkling wine

325g (11oz) caster sugar

3 sprigs of basil

For the confit orange zest
zest of 7 oranges, removed in strips with a vegetable peeler

200g (7oz) sugar

500ml (17fl oz) water

For the orange syrup
juice of 7 oranges

50g (2oz) sugar

1 vanilla pod, split open lengthways and seeds scraped out

1 star anise

1 cinnamon stick

2 cloves

Put the berries, mint and Pimm's in a bowl, stir lightly and set aside for at least 20 minutes.

Place the gelatine in a bowl of cold water and leave to soak for 10 minutes.

Meanwhile, place the wine, sugar and basil in a saucepan over a low heat and stir until the sugar has dissolved. Squeeze any excess moisture out of the gelatine, then add to the wine mixture and stir until dissolved. Strain the Pimm's into the pan, stir and set aside to cool for about 30 minutes or until it reaches room temperature.

Divide half the drained berries between nine 175ml (6fl oz) dariole moulds or ramekins. Half-fill the dishes with the wine mixture and refrigerate until set (about 1 hour). Once set, divide the remaining berries between the dishes and top up with the wine mixture. Refrigerate until set (about 1 hour).

To prepare the confit, finely slice the strips of zest. Put the sugar and water in a small pan and heat until the sugar has dissolved. Add the zest and simmer gently until soft.

To make the orange syrup, strain the orange juice into a saucepan. Add the sugar, vanilla pod and seeds, star anise, cinnamon and cloves. Place over a gentle heat to dissolve the sugar, then bring to the boil and simmer until the mixture coats back of spoon, skimming off any scum that forms on the surface. When the mixture coats the back of a spoon, strain and set aside to cool.

For the tuiles (makes about 20)

115g (3¾oz) butter

125g (4oz) caster sugar

about 4 egg whites (125–135g/ 4–4½oz in total)

115g (3¾oz) plain flour

sesame seeds

To make the tuiles, preheat the oven to 160°C/325°F/Gas Mark 3.

Put the butter and sugar in a bowl and beat until light and fluffy. Add the egg whites, a little at a time, mixing thoroughly after each addition. Add the flour and mix again.

Using a palette knife, spread the mixture thinly into rectangles on a silicone baking mat. We do this using a rectangular template cut out of a thin plastic sheet (such as the plastic lid of an ice cream tub) to shape ours.

Sprinkle each tuile with ½ tsp sesame seeds, then bake for about 4 minutes, or until golden. Keep an eye on them, as they cook very fast. (The tuiles keep for ages and can be crisped up in the oven for a minute.)

To serve, place the darioles in hot water for 2 seconds, then invert on to serving plates. Garnish with the extra berries and mint leaves, sprinkle with the confit orange zest and drizzle over the orange syrup. Serve with the sesame tuiles.

Sheila Hitchon has adapted her granny's recipe to create this wonderful dessert. The damsons she uses come from her family farm in Herefordshire – the same trees her granny picked fruit from – and Sheila makes her own damson gin with them too. Sloe gin also works well in the recipe.

DAMSON PUDDING

SERVES 8–10

675g (1lb 6oz) damsons

150g (5oz) caster sugar

250ml (8fl oz) double cream

500g (1lb) mascarpone cheese

125g (4oz) icing sugar, sifted

285g (9½oz) Madeira cake, cut into 2.5cm (1in) cubes

about 150ml (¼ pint) damson or sloe gin

about 150ml (¼ pint) whipping cream

Preheat the oven to 160°C/325°F/Gas Mark 3.

Place the damsons in an ovenproof dish and bake for 15–20 minutes, until soft enough to remove the stones easily. Stir the caster sugar into the stoned fruit, then transfer to a blender and whiz to a purée. Pass the mixture through a sieve, discard the solids and set aside until cold.

Mix the cream and mascarpone together in a large bowl. Add the icing sugar and mix until smooth.

Arrange the cake cubes in a single layer in a shallow dish, drizzle with the gin and set aside to soak in.

In a deep glass bowl that holds about 2.75 litres/5 pints, pour in a third of the damson purée. Arrange half the cake cubes over the surface, then spread with half the mascarpone mixture. Add another third of the damson purée, the rest of the cake and the remaining mascarpone. Top with the last of the purée, then cover and chill for at least 6 hours, but preferably overnight.

Just before serving, whip the whipping cream into stiff peaks, spoon into a piping bag and pipe a lattice pattern over the top of the pudding.

Betty Moore's apple pie recipe has already earned her a bronze medal at the Melton Mowbray British Pie Awards. She uses Bramley apples from her cottage garden, and although she has experimented with different kinds of pastry, Betty finds that her own homemade shortcrust is the best.

FAMILY APPLE PIE

SERVES 6

1kg (2lb) Bramley apples, peeled, cored and roughly chopped

2 tsp caster sugar (or to taste), plus extra for dusting

1 tbsp milk for brushing

For the pastry
125g (4oz) plain flour, plus extra for dusting

125g (4oz) self-raising flour

pinch of salt

125g (4oz) butter

25g (1oz) lard

150ml (¼ pint) water

Preheat the oven to 180°C/350°F/Gas Mark 4.

First make the pastry. Place the flours, salt and fats in a bowl and rub together or process until the mixture resembles breadcrumbs. Add the water very gradually, until a dough forms. Wrap in cling film and place in the fridge for 15–20 minutes.

Meanwhile, put the apples in a saucepan and add just enough water to come three-quarters of the way up them. Cover and bring to the boil, then take off the heat. Turn the apples so that those on top are moved to the bottom, put the lid back on and set aside to cool. Drain carefully. You want the apples to be soft but still holding their shape.

On a lightly floured work surface, roll out half the pastry to the thickness of two £1 coins and use it to line a deep pie dish, about 18cm (7in) in diameter. Put the cooked apples in the pastry case and sprinkle with the sugar. Roll out the remaining pastry and use to cover the apples. Trim off the excess, then crimp the edges together using fingers and thumb. Make a slit in the top of the pie for steam to escape.

Brush the pie with the milk and bake for 30–35 minutes, until the pastry is golden. Dust with sugar and serve with ice cream or custard.

Part-time primary school teacher Liz Hughes also runs a vegetarian cookery school, and has adapted the classic Malvern Pudding recipe to be vegan, as well as dairy- and gluten-free. Malvern is famous for its apples, so naturally Liz sources all of hers locally when she makes this dish.

LIZ'S MALVERN PUDDING

SERVES 4

25g (1oz) margarine

450g (14½oz) cooking apples, peeled, cored and sliced

zest of ½ lemon

25g (1oz) sugar

For the custard

2 tbsp custard powder

2 tbsp sugar

600ml (1 pint) soya milk

For the topping

3 tbsp demerara sugar

1 tsp ground cinnamon

15g (½oz) margarine, chopped into small pieces

Melt the margarine in a pan. Add the apples, lemon zest and sugar and cook until the apples are just soft. Place them in a shallow oval baking dish (about 25 x 20cm/10 x 8in).

To make the custard, put the custard powder and sugar into a heatproof bowl or large jug, add a small amount of the milk and mix to a paste.

Heat the remaining milk in a saucepan until nearly boiling, then pour it into the paste, stirring well. Return the mixture to the saucepan, place over a high heat and bring to the boil, stirring continuously. Simmer for 2 minutes, until the custard thickens, then pour it over the apples.

Preheat the grill to high.

To make the topping, combine the demerara sugar and cinnamon in a small bowl, then sprinkle the mixture over the custard. Dot the margarine over the top and cook the pudding under the grill until it bubbles and the sugar is caramelised. Serve hot or cold.

Celebration cake-maker Tracy Brookes adds pears to the classic Bakewell Tart recipe handed down through her family – it is one of the first desserts she can remember baking as a child. Her granddad has a lot of pear trees and always gives her family bagfuls of pears when they visit, so they are in abundant supply.

BAKEWELL TART

SERVES 8

225g (7½oz) caster sugar

225g (7½oz) margarine

4 eggs

115g (3¾oz) self-raising flour

115g (3¾oz) ground almonds

200g (7oz) homemade or best-quality raspberry jam

handful of flaked almonds

icing sugar for dusting

For the pastry
175g (6oz) plain flour, plus extra for dusting

65g (2½ oz) butter

35g (1¼oz) lard

3-5 tablespoons water

For the pears
200g (7oz) caster sugar

1 vanilla pod, split open lengthways and seeds scraped out

300 ml (½ pint) water

1-2 ripe pears, peeled, cored and halved

First make the pastry. Put the flour, butter and lard into a bowl and rub together or pulse until the mixture resembles breadcrumbs. Stir in the water a little at a time, until a smooth dough forms. Wrap in cling film and place in the fridge for at least 15 minutes.

Preheat the oven to 200°C/400°F/Gas Mark 6.

On a lightly floured work surface, roll out the pastry to a thickness of 5mm (¼in) and use to line a 23cm (9in) tart tin. (I like to use a fluted tin because it makes the pastry crisper on the outside.) Prick the base several times with a fork, then line the pastry case with crumpled greaseproof paper, ensuring it overhangs the edges. Fill with ceramic baking beans or uncooked pulses or rice and bake for 20 minutes, until just starting to brown. Remove the paper and beans and return to the oven for another 5 minutes to dry out.

While the pastry case is baking, prepare the pears. Put the sugar, vanilla pod and seeds and water in a saucepan and heat until the sugar dissolves. Add the pears and cook on a really low simmer for about 20 minutes, until soft to the point of a knife. Using a slotted spoon, transfer the pears to a plate and set aside. When cool, cut into slices about 5mm (¼in) thick.

Reduce the oven temperature to 150°C/300°F/Gas Mark 2.

To make the filling, put the sugar and margarine in a bowl and beat together until pale and fluffy. Mix in the eggs one at a time, either

by hand or on a slow mixer setting, beating in 1 tablespoon of flour between each egg to prevent the mixture from curdling. Sift in the remaining flour, stir well, then mix in the ground almonds. Take care not to overmix: stop when you have a smooth batter.

Spread the jam inside the pastry case and arrange the pears evenly on top. Carefully spread the almond filling over the pears and bake in the middle of the oven for 25 minutes. Sprinkle the flaked almonds over the tart and return to the oven for another 10 minutes or so, until golden brown and well risen.

Set aside until warm (or cold if you prefer), then dust lightly with icing sugar and serve. I like to eat the tart with a dollop of thick cream.

SONIA'S TIPSY TART

SERVES 6-8

175g (6oz) dates, chopped

1 tsp bicarbonate of soda

175ml (6fl oz) boiling water

150g (5oz) plain flour

¼ tsp baking powder

¼ tsp salt

35-65g (1¼-2½oz) mixed chopped nuts

2 scant tbsp butter, plus extra for greasing

200g (7oz) granulated sugar

1 egg

For the sauce

300g (10oz) granulated sugar

175ml (6fl oz) water

1 tbsp butter

1 tsp vanilla extract

50ml (2fl oz) brandy, such as Klipdrift

Preheat the oven to 190°C/375°F/Gas Mark 5. Butter two 20cm (8in) loose-bottomed tart tins.

Put the dates in a bowl. Mix the bicarbonate of soda with the boiling water in a heatproof jug and pour this liquid over the dates. Set aside to soak for at least 30 minutes.

Sift the flour, baking powder and salt into a bowl and stir in the chopped nuts.

Put the butter, sugar and egg in a bowl and beat together. Gradually add the flour mixture, beating between each addition. Stir in the dates.

Divide the mixture between the prepared tins and bake for 25-30 minutes, until the tops spring back when pressed lightly. Allow to cool in the tins for 10 minutes, then turn out and transfer to a wire rack.

To make the sauce, put the sugar and water in a pan and boil for 5 minutes, stirring constantly until the sugar has dissolved. Add the butter and boil for a further 3-4 minutes, until fairly thick. Stir in the vanilla extract and brandy. Pour the syrup over the tarts and serve with whipped cream.

STRAWBERRY & DARK CHOCOLATE CHEESECAKE

SERVES 12

400g (13oz) mascarpone cheese

115g (3¾oz) icing sugar, sifted

**2 vanilla pods, split open
lengthways and seeds scraped out**

300ml (½ pint) double cream

**½ punnet of strawberries, hulled
and sliced**

dark chocolate, to decorate

For the base
75g (3oz) unsalted butter

**175g (6oz) chocolate chip
cookies, crushed**

Line the base of a shallow 23cm (9in) springform cake tin with baking parchment.

To make the base, melt the butter in a saucepan and mix in the biscuit crumbs. Tip into the prepared tin and press down firmly and evenly with the back of a spoon. Place in the freezer while you make the filling.

Put the mascarpone in a bowl and mix in the icing sugar and vanilla seeds. Whip the cream into soft peaks, then fold into the mascarpone mixture.

Remove the biscuit base from the freezer and spoon the filling over it. Tap the tin on the work surface to remove any air pockets, then place in the fridge for at least 2 hours.

Unmould the cheesecake from the tin and transfer to a serving plate. Decorate the top with the sliced strawberries and dark chocolate shavings or curls.

Thomas Blandford loves to cook, and has been helping his mum in the kitchen since he was little. He tried lots of different flavour combinations with cheesecake before deciding that strawberry and dark chocolate was his favourite. Thomas prefers to use Welsh butter for the base, but any unsalted butter will do.

Index

Acknowledgements

A huge thank you to all the wonderful *Food Glorious Food* contestants.

SYCO
SIMON COWELL
NIGEL HALL
MICHAEL JOCHNOWITZ
CAROLE DAVIDS
NAOMI EDLER

OPTOMEN
PAT LLEWELLYN
BEN ADLER
SUE MURPHY
BECKY CLARKE
SARAH DURDIN ROBERTSON

ITV
ELAINE BEDELL
ASIF ZUBAIRY

MARKS & SPENCER
STEVE SHARP
ADELE WOODS

PICTURE CREDITS

Felicity Crawshaw 1 top left & bottom centre, 2, 10 centre, 102, 105, 106, 110, 112, 113, 114, 115, 117, 118, 122, 123, 124, 125, 126, 127, 128, 129, 130, 131, 132, 133, 134, 135, 136, 137, 142, 144, 145, 147, 148, 150, 151, 152, 153, 154, 157, 158, 159, 160, 164, 166, 167 above, 169, 170, 172, 173, 176, 178-179, 214 below left.

Andrew Hayes-Watkins 1 (all except top left & bottom centre), 10 (all except centre), 12, 15, 22, 33, 38, 42, 44 (all except below right), 52, 64, 66, 69, 70, 71, 73, 76, 77, 82, 83, 87, 88, 90, 92, 95, 96, 99, 182, 187, 196, 202, 205, 207, 209, 214 (all except below left), 225, 227, 231, 235, 236, 237, 238, 239, 247.

Maidmetal Ltd 16, 19, 20, 24, 26, 28, 34, 37, 41, 46, 51, 54, 57 below, 59, 60, 68, 74, 78, 81, 84, 89, 94, 98, 104, 139, 162, 174, 184, 186, 188, 190, 192, 197, 198, 200, 204, 206, 208, 210, 216, 219, 220, 223, 224, 228, 230, 233, 234, 241, 242, 245, 246.

Octopus Publishing Group/William Shaw 4-5, 13, 14, 17, 18, 21, 23, 25, 27, 30-31, 32, 35, 36, 39, 40, 43, 44 below right, 48-49, 50, 53, 55, 57 above, 58, 61, 67, 72, 75, 79, 81, 85, 91, 93, 108-109, 111, 116, 120-121, 138, 146, 155, 156, 163, 167 below, 168, 171, 175, 185, 189, 191, 194-195, 199, 201, 203, 211, 217, 218, 221, 222, 226, 229, 232, 240, 243, 244.

Syco/James Breeden 6.

Various background images throughout: **Thinkstock**.

Illustrations: **Jonny Hannah**

FOOD Glorious FOOD

First published in Great Britain in 2013
by Mitchell Beazley,
an imprint of Octopus Publishing Group Limited,
Endeavour House, 189 Shaftesbury Avenue,
London, WC2H 8JY
www.octopusbooks.co.uk

An Hachette UK Company
www.hachette.co.uk

ISBN: 978-1-84533-813-8

A CIP catalogue record for this book is available from the
British Library

Printed and bound in Italy

Publishing Director: Stephanie Jackson
Managing Editor: Clare Churly
Editor: Patricia Burgess
Editorial contributors: Jane Birch & Katy Denny

Art Director & Book Design: Jonathan Christie
Illustrator: Jonny Hannah

Photography Art Director: Isabel De Cordova
Photographer: William Shaw
Home economist: Sara Lewis
Home economist's assistant: Andrew Lewis
Stylist: Liz Belton

Picture Research Manager: Giulia Hetherington

Senior Production Manager: Peter Hunt

Both metric and imperial measurements are given for
the recipes. Use one set of measures only, not a mixture
of both.

Standard level spoon measurements are used in all recipes:
1 tablespoon = 15 ml
1 teaspoon = 5 ml

Ovens should be preheated to the specified temperature. If
using a fan-assisted oven, follow the manufacturer's
instructions for adjusting the time and temperature.
Grills should also be preheated.

This book includes dishes made with nuts and nut derivatives.
It is advisable for those with known allergic reactions to nuts
and nut derivatives and those who may be potentially
vulnerable to these allergies, such as pregnant and nursing
mothers, invalids, the elderly, babies and children, to avoid
dishes made with nuts and nut oils. It is also prudent to check
the labels of preprepared ingredients for the possible
inclusion of nut derivatives.

The Department of Health advises that eggs should not be
consumed raw. This book contains some dishes made with
raw or lightly cooked eggs. It is prudent for more vulnerable
people such as pregnant and nursing mothers, invalids, the
elderly, babies and young children to avoid uncooked or
lightly cooked dishes made with eggs.